# WHAT PEOPLE ARE SAYING ABOUT THE ONE ANOTHERING SERIES

"Dick Meyer's *One Anothering* series offers small groups the chance to grow together by both explanation and experience. His unique writing presents reflection on the small group process (from a skilled facilitator) and calls us to serious sharing on personal and spiritual levels. The third volume, *Creating Significant Spiritual Community*, delivers on the promise. This book really can foster spiritual community in your small group."
> —Dr. Charles Denison, Dougans and Denison, New Church Development Consulting

"Can another book on small groups be too much of a good thing? Absolutely not! With captivating stories and insightful biblical analysis, Meyer builds on his previous work to reveal deeper dimensions of intentional community life."
> —Rev. Ann Jahnes, St. Andrews Covenant Presbyterian Church, Wilmington, NC

"We have used Dick Meyer's ONE ANOTHERING books with our small groups over the last eight years and have experienced life-changing results personally and in our church."
> —Rev. Charles F. Scott and Ms. Mary Scott, Ministers-at-Large for Young Life, South-Central Division

"An excellent resource . . . provides life-giving experiential ways to grow within small faith communities . . . one of the most practical small group resources used in our ecumenical Institute of Small Group Development."
> —Hal Edwards, President, Christian Laity of Chicago

"If you are looking to turn your church or company into a community of caring people, I know of no better place to get started than this."
> —Lyman Coleman, President, Serendipity House

"I can't wait to put this book into the hands of every one of our small group leaders. Once again Dick Meyer has brought his marvelous experience to bear on one of our most pressing needs—growing community through small groups."
> —E. Stanley Ott, President, The Vital Church Institute

"Dick Meyer sets the playing field, outlines the game rules, and tosses hittable batting practice for small groups who want to work on their relational game. With clear, simple, accessible, and practical coaching, he guides small groups into the depth and complexity of biblical life together. With a stadium full of great stories, he helps reform rough-hewn gatherings into sparkling communal diamonds. Truly a disciple's guide to good groups."
  —Gareth Icenogle, author, pastor, and adjunct professor

"A down-to-earth look at what it means to live together in spiritual community . . . if depth and vitality are what your group needs, this book is a must."
  —Rev. Charlie Ayars, Clear Lake Presbyterian Church, Houston

"Inspiring, insightful, and most importantly, useful . . . Dick Meyer is the best small group facilitator I know in this country."
  —Rev. Dennis Denning, Northminster Presbyterian Church, Cincinnati

*One Anothering, Volume 3*

# One Anothering
## Volume 3

*Creating*
*Significant*
*Spiritual*
*Community*

*Richard C. Meyer*

**Augsburg Books**
MINNEAPOLIS

ONE ANOTHERING, VOLUME 3
Creating Significant Spiritual Community

Large-quantity purchases or custom editions of this book are available at a discount from the publisher. For more information, contact the sales department at Augsburg Fortress, Publishers, 1-800-328-4648, or write to: Sales Director, Augsburg Fortress, Publishers, P. O. Box 1209, Minneapolis, MN 55440-1209.

ISBN 0-8066-9057-7

Cover art by Michael Littlewood-Biddison. © 1998 Michael Biddison. All rights reserved.

Manufactured in the U.S.A.

09   08   07   06   05   1   2   3   4   5   6   7   8   9   10

*To Barc Wade, Pat Minard, and Marjory Bankson*

*who first invited me to write.*

# Contents

*To my editor, Marcia Broucek,*
*for her wise, encouraging, and honest counsel.*

*To the Faith at Work community*
*who gave me my first opportunity to write.*

*To all the wonderful men and women*
*with whom I have been blessed to be in a small group,*
*and who have given me so many wonderful stories to tell.*

*To the West Hills Presbyterian Church in Omaha, Nebraska,*
*the Brookings Presbyterian Church in Oregon,*
*and the First Presbyterian Church of Maitland*
*who allowed me to do my "small group thing" in their midst.*

*To my wife, Trudy, who has never doubted my ability to write.*

# INTRODUCTION

I love small groups. I have made being in a small group a spiritual discipline in my life for the past thirty years. Wherever we have lived, and we have lived in a number of places, I have asked others to join me in building intentional spiritual community. I am glad I did. By participating in small groups, I have made life-long friends, been challenged spiritually, and I have gained a greater awareness of Jesus Christ in daily life. I have been in great small groups, and I have been in not so great small groups, and over the years I have learned from experience—sometimes painful—what facilitates community and what impedes community. What I write comes out of my personal experience as well as the New Testament Scriptures.

This book marks the third, and final, volume in the One Anothering series. As in previous volumes, I have taken "one another" passages from the New Testament, reflected on them, and written group discussion and sharing questions for each of them. If you are new to the series, know that the volumes do not need to be studied in order. Each volume stands on its own. Also know that brand new groups can use this book as a "starter course," or veteran groups can use it as a "refresher course" in small group basics.

As you begin your group, or as you continue your group experience, keep the following group guidelines in mind. They will make your small group experience more enjoyable.

*Cultivate healthy participation patterns.*

Some people have a tendency to dominate a conversation. Others seldom speak. As a result, we may hear more from some group members than others. Some of this can be remedied by having group members take turns sharing. That way, everyone has time to talk. Still, the extroverts may talk way more than the introverts in the group. How do we deal with this problem of unequalized participation?

First, we accept the natural differences in people. Some people are naturally more talkative than others. As a result, group participation will never be totally equal. Second, as leaders we choose our seat carefully. Sitting next to a talkative person or across from a quiet person works wonders.

Take the "icebreaker," for example. As group leaders, we want to sit next to the talkative person to help "tone down" that individual. We can start the sharing in the direction away from the talkative person. With the talkative person on our right, we check-in first and then go to the person on our left and proceed around the circle until we finally come to Talkative Ted. By the time it is Ted's time to talk, everyone else has had time to share. We also sit next to Ted to cut off our "non-verbals" to him. Without Ted being able to see our non-verbal nods and winks, he is less likely to share as much.

Of course, the opposite is true of the less verbal member. With the Silent Sally of the group, we want to sit across from her. We want to give the silent members gobs of non-verbal encouragement. As they talk, we want to lean forward, smile, nod, and wink. We want to invite them to say more, and if our non-verbal efforts do not get the job done, we want to invite them verbally to talk more. We say things like, "Sally, tell me more," or "Sally, how did that feel?" or "Sally, what do you think about that?"

*Keep confidences.*

Few things destroy a group faster than broken confidentiality. A group gains confidence if it *keeps* confidences.

I think of the eight-year-old boy who was playing beside an open window while a neighbor confided to his mother about another person. When the visitor was gone, the mother, realizing how much her son had overheard, called him to her side. "If Mrs. Brown had left her purse just now, would you give it to someone else?

"Of course not!" the lad replied.

"Ah," the mother commented, "Mrs. Brown left something more precious than her purse. The story she told could hurt many people and cause much unhappiness. It still belongs to her, and we shall not pass it along to anyone."

Groups who keep things to themselves provide a safe place for people to share their hopes, dreams, frustrations, and hurts. They know to pass that information along to others will destroy that safe haven. A portion of the Hippocratic Oath comes to mind: "And whatsoever I shall see or hear in the course of my profession . . . if it be what should not be published abroad, I will never divulge, holding such things to be holy secrets."

Each week in a group, holy secrets are shared, and if a confidence is broken, it needs to be addressed swiftly and directly. The person who broke the confidence needs to be confronted, and assurances need to be given that such a thing will not happen again. If such assurances cannot be given, the person needs to be asked to leave the group. Better to lose one person than to lose an entire group.

*Refrain from fixing and advice giving.*

I still remember the attorney in our group. When we suggested that we were to refrain from fixing and advice giving in the group, he was troubled. After all, that is how he helped people. They came to him because they had a problem. They sought his legal counsel and advice. "If someone in the group shares a problem and we are not to give advice, then what are we to do?" he asked.

We are to *care*, not *cure*. If people want advice, they are to request it. Until they do, we simply listen and allow the Holy Spirit to do the curing. The Apostle Paul put it well when he wrote, "I planted, Apollos watered, but God gave the growth" (1 Corinthians 3:6). We listen, we care, but God does the curing.

Advice giving has its problems. First, it places the advice giver in a superior position, dispensing wisdom from on high. When I share a problem, I do not necessarily want advice. I want someone to listen to me, and I hope they empathize with me. When someone gives me unsolicited advice, I often feel as if I am being talked down to. If I wanted their advice, I would have asked for it. I think of a woman with her husband. She said, "Every time I tell him a problem, he tells me how to fix it. He makes me feel so dumb." That is one of the risks of being an advice giver. We place ourselves in a superior position of having "the answer." Second, advice giving assumes we know the entire story, and often we do not. To give advice without knowing the details is potentially foolhardy and dangerous. How often have we heard someone say, "I took your advice, and this is what happened. I never should have listened to you!" Third, being a "fix it" type of group places pressure on the group to come up with "good advice." If we realize, however, that we are the caregivers and God is the Curegiver, it relieves the pressure. We do not have to fix the problem. That is God's job. We can relax and listen.

When someone shares a problem in the group, it is better to say, "That sounds tough; how can we be praying for you?" or "I am sorry to hear that; is there anything specific we can do?" If they seek some specific advice, they will ask for it. If not, we have prepared the ground for the great Curegiver to work.

*Face the inevitable.*

Groups do not stay together forever. When a group first forms, there is often a hope that the group will always be together. That rarely, if ever, happens. People come and go in groups. Life situations change. Enthusiasm wanes. People move. Commitment sags. For these reasons, and others, the make-up of a group changes. While the average life span of a small group is two years, some groups go on indefinitely. A group I joined in 1975 continues to meet. Of the original twelve, only two remain (I left in 1990). The group has survived by inviting new people into the group. These new folk have infused the group with fresh enthusiasm. The group has also maintained positive relationships with those who left the group because of the way they handled the leaving. That is, they viewed it more as a "sending" than a "leaving." Once a year they invite their "group alumni" to a barbecue as a way of keeping in touch with one another.

* * *

My first small group experience came in seminary in 1971. I joined the group reluctantly. I was required to attend. My grade depended on it. That experience, however, changed me life. May it change yours. May God bless you and your group as you work through the "one another" passages in this concluding *One Anothering* volume.

# CHAPTER ONE

# BELONG TO ONE ANOTHER

So in Christ we who are many
form one body with many members,
and each member belongs to all the others.
Romans 12:5 NIV

We are members of one another.
Ephesians 2:25

B enjamin Franklin wrote it. Just about everyone can quote it:

"Early to bed, early to rise,
Makes a person healthy, wealthy, and wise."

"Morning" people certainly affirm the wisdom of this proverb. At least, it gives "morning" people an answer to the question, "Why do you go to bed so early?" Contrary to what others may think (i.e., my children), "morning" people, like me, are not "fuddy-duddies." Rather we like to think we are taking better care of ourselves by observing a conservative, responsible lifestyle. We do not waste our energy watching late night television or partying until sunup. We tuck ourselves in by 10 PM so we will be ready for the day at dawn.

Of course, "night" people think the proverb is a bunch of hooey. They believe old Ben Franklin was a "morning" person. They reject the proverb. They claim, "It's not how early you go to bed, or how early you get up in the morning, that contributes to success. It has more to do with energy, creativity, and industry. Night people can be just as energetic and creative and industrious as morning people. We just do it at a different time of day."

I suspect they are right. Are morning people healthier, wealthier, and wiser than night people? I doubt it. I suspect the proverb would wilt under close examination.

There is something, however, that *does* make us healthier, wealthier, and wiser. That something is a sense of belonging. Research bears this out. Simply put: Deepen your relational connections and you will improve your life. Robert Putnam, Professor of Public Policy at Harvard University asks,

> Does social capital (connections between individuals) have salutary effects on individuals, communities, or even entire nations? Yes, an impressive growing body of research suggests that civic connections help make us healthy, wealthy, and wise. Living without social capital is not easy, whether one is a villager in southern Italy or a poor person in the American inner city or a well-healed entrepreneur in a high-tech industrial district.[1]

## BECOMING HEALTHY, WEALTHY, AND WISE

Does belonging make us healthier? You bet. Research shows that people rich in relationships handle stress better, have a stronger immune system, have lower blood pressure, and are two to five times less likely to die from all causes compared to those with weak relational ties.[2] The research prompted one expert to write,

> As a rough rule of thumb, if you belong to no groups but decide to join one, you cut your risk of dying over the next year in half. If you smoke and belong to no groups, it's a toss-up statistically whether you should stop smoking or start joining. These findings are in some ways heartening: it's easier to join a group than to lose weight, exercise regularly, or quit smoking.[3]

Does belonging also make us wealthier? Yes, it does! Remember the old saying, "It's not what you know, but who you know?" Apparently, it possesses an element of truth. Having strong relational ties certainly opens economic doors. For example, the unemployed often look to friends, family, and acquaintances in finding job leads, with good results. One-half of them get their jobs through such relational sources. Belonging, however, not only helps us find employment, but also saves us money. Join an organization such as the American Automobile Association or the American Association of Retired Persons or Costco or your company's credit union, and you receive discounts on travel, entertainment, food, insurance, and loans. Joining a group—be it a small group or a large group—may not turn you into a Bill Gates or a Warren Buffet, but it may put more money in your pocket.

Finally, does belonging make us wiser? Again, the answer is yes. A good number of my childhood friends went to parochial school. They attended Holy Family Elementary School, and nuns instructed them. Did they receive a better education, than I received? I cannot say, but I can relay a research study done of Catholic schools in the Chicago metropolitan area. The conclusion to the study read, "Catholic schools do better than public schools not because the teachers or students are more qualified but because Catholic schools benefit from a network of social relations."[4] The parents, teachers, and administrators have an element of trust toward one another not found in the average Chicago public school. They feel they are in this together. They feel they are part of the child's learning "team." Thus, children in Catholic schools do better on standardized tests. In a similar vain, studies have also shown that smaller schools tend to outperform larger schools because small schools give students more opportunities to engage face-to-face.[5] In other words, we learn best in a trusting, face-to-face environment, rich in social capital.

Going to bed and rising early may not make us healthy, wealthy, and wise, but developing deep, supportive relationships will. The Apostle Paul knew this intuitively when he wrote, "So in Christ we who are many form one body with many members, and each member belongs to all the others" (Romans 12:5 NIV).

## A NEW AGE IN CHRIST

Paul's words come on the heels of a lengthy theological discussion on how to be "reconciled to Christ." After spending eleven chapters on this very important subject, he moves to application. He turns from doctrine to ethics. He turns his attention from how to be reconciled in Christ to how to function in everyday life. For Paul, Jesus Christ ushered in a new age, and in the remaining chapters, he outlines how Christians ought to conduct themselves in this new age.

I recall when I decided to get married. I knew how I lived in the "old age" (my single days) would not work in the "new age" (married life). I had to switch from a "me" to a "we" orientation toward life. In the "me" days, I could watch sports all day long, wash the sheets when they looked dirty (once a month), and go out with my friends whenever the mood struck. In the "me" days I looked out for myself, no one else. The new "we" days demanded something else—for the better! The "we" days required me to hone my listening skills, to run things by my "another" before making a decision, and to do some things that were not necessarily on my list of top ten things to do. I do these things because I want to spend the rest of my life with the love of my life, and I much prefer the new age (marriage) to the old age (being single). Now, I know some prefer just the opposite. Some prefer singleness to marriage, and I am not for a minute saying that one state is better than another. All I am saying is that for me, marriage works better than singleness. Having met "Ms. Right," I want to continue to live in this "new" age.

The same applies to my relationship with Christ. I became a follower of Christ when I was in college, and I much prefer the new age to the old age. I much prefer being "in" Christ than being "without" Christ. I much prefer knowing God than being apart from God. I much prefer knowing that God is near rather than far off. I much prefer knowing God loves me rather than hoping God loves me. I enjoy this "new" age, but it demands things of me that the "old" age did not, and Paul outlines these things at the end of his letter to the Romans. One of these demands is to live in community with other followers of Christ. For Paul, being in Christ has a vertical and a horizontal dimension. In the eyes of Paul, when we come to Christ, we not only become reconciled to God, but also to every other individual who says, "Yes," to Christ. The image Paul employs is that of a human body:

> Just as each of us has one body with many members,
> and these members do not all have the same function,
> so in Christ we who are many form one body, and each
> member belongs to all the others. (Romans 12:4-5 NIV)

## THE BODY OF CHRIST

What a great metaphor the body is! Everyone can relate to it because everyone has one. We experience our body everyday. Some days our body works great, and some days not so great. Some days we feel like a million bucks, and some days it feels as if we got hit by a million trucks. We know about bodies.

We also know how much we want our body to function properly. Dealing with a breaking-down body tests our patience and state of mind. Someone once said, "You know you're getting older when everything hurts, and what doesn't hurt, doesn't work!" One does not need to get older, however, to realize how much each body part means to our well being. A toothache, a stomach cramp, or a sprained ankle remind us that it does not take much for a body part to grab our attention. I recently joined a health club and participated in the "Body Pump" class that consisted of doing exercises with weights. It seemed tame enough. You can use as little or as many weights as you like while you do knee bends, lunges, and curls to music. The next day I could hardly walk down stairs, my thighs hurt so much. Each body part is important!

Moreover, body parts need each other. My lungs need my heart to pump blood to them. My muscles need my brain to send messages to them. My fingers need my muscles to bend properly, and my stomach needs my throat to swallow nutrients. My hand cannot say to my arm, "I don't need you." My heart cannot say to my lungs, "I don't need you." My eyes cannot say to my eyelids, "I don't need you." Without my arm, my hand could not reach. Without my lungs, my heart would not pump. Without my eyelids, my eyes would not be able to see.

So it goes in the Body of Christ. In this metaphor Paul underscores how much we need one another. Two millenniums before Dr. Putnam's insights on the importance of social connections, Paul clearly tells us that we function better together than apart. According to Paul, when we separate ourselves from each other, we cease to function as we were intended to function. We are like a body without a hand. We can do without a hand, but we function much better with one.

Christ ushered in a new age of community, a new age of belonging. Paul urges us to live into this age. He wants us to affirm our dependence on one another, but to do so requires us to let go of some old age ways of thinking. Why do so many resist developing significant relationships with other followers of Christ? I mentioned three reasons in *One Anothering, Volume 2:* ignorance, time, and fear. Some do not join a group because they are unaware of the benefits of being in a small group. They do not know how much a small group can come to mean in their lives. Others do not join a group because of time constraints. Trying to fit another meeting, another commitment into an already packed schedule seems impossible. Finally, there is the fear factor. The fear varies from person to person. Some fear having to share more of themselves than they are ready to share. Others fear that being in a group will reveal their lack of knowledge about the Bible, and still others fear being asked to pray out loud in a group. These three things—ignorance, time, fear—keep many from joining a small group. Something else, however, keeps people apart. Old age thinking characterized by individualism, selfishness, and self-sufficiency contributes to people thinking "me" rather than "we."

## OLD AGE THINKING

*The first characteristic of old age thinking is INDIVIDUALISM.*
Alexis de Tocqueville, in the early nineteenth century, described individualism as our culture's primary operative:

> Individualism is a calm and considered feeling which disposes each citizen to isolate himself from the mass of his fellows and withdraw into the circle of family and friends; with this little society formed to his taste, he gladly leaves the greater society to look after itself . . . They form the habit if thinking of themselves in isolation and imagine that their whole destiny is in their hands . . . Each man is forever thrown back on himself alone, and there is danger that he may shut up in the solitude of his own heart.[6]

We see this illustrated in the words of our nation's forebears. Thomas Jefferson said, "I am a sect myself," and Thomas Paine said, "My mind is my church."[7] Herbert Hoover, in his book *The Challenge of Liberty*, wrote, "While I can make no claim for having introduced the term, 'rugged individualism,' I should be proud to have invented it. It has been used by American leaders for over a half-century in eulogy of those God-fearing men and women of honesty whose stamina and character and fearless assertion of rights led them to make their own way in life.[8]

This individualistic mind set remains with us today. I think back to my father's funeral. He died a number of years ago from a massive heart attack. We traveled from Omaha, Nebraska, to Reno, Nevada, to attend the services. He had made arrangements with a local funeral home prior to his death, and he requested a song to be sung at his funeral service. The song? I could hardly keep a straight face when the funeral director informed my sister and me of his choice. My father wanted us to play Frank Sinatra's "I Did It My Way." Of course, that song captured our father. Without having gone to college, and without the help of his parents, he worked himself up the economic ladder, from a New Jersey farm boy to vice-president of a large savings and loan. He did it his way, and he was proud of his accomplishments. He was a tough, stubborn Marine. He consumed Louis L'Amour novels. He loved westerns where the cowboy rides into town alone on his trusty horse, and with a six-shooter in hand captures the villain and rides out of town, once again alone, into the sunset. His hero was John Wayne, as rugged and strong as they come.

We swim in a culture of individualism. We want to be free to come and go as we please. We don't want anyone impinging on us or invading our space. The idea of car pooling or riding public transportation seems like an infringement on our freedom. It even spills over into matters of faith. Sociologist Robert Bellah and his colleagues in their stellar work *Habits of the Heart: Individualism and Commitment in American Life* tell of a young nurse named Sheila. Sheila describes her faith as "Sheilaism." She says, "I believe in God. I'm not a religious fanatic. I can't remember the last time I went to church. My faith has carried me a long way. It's Sheilaism. Just my own little voice."[9]

Sociologists refer to "individualistic" cultures and "collectivistic" cultures. We Americans live in an individualistic culture. Individualistic cultures value individual achievement and recognition over team achievement and recognition. They promote self-actualization, encouraging individuals to be all they can be. The United States, Great Britain, and Australia top the list of individualistic cultures. Collectivistic cultures, on the other hand, value just the opposite. Cultures such as Japan, China, Venezuela, and Pakistan value group achievement over individual achievement. They think of the group as the primary unit of society, whereas individualistic cultures think of the individual as the primary unit. To them, "we" is more important than "me."

The Apostle Paul encourages us to move from an individualistic mind set to a collectivistic mind set. He encourages us to move from a "me" to a "we." He reminds us that in Christ we are members of one another. We are not islands unto ourselves, but rather parts of a body, connected to each other. When we turn from the old age to the new age, we change our tune from "I Did It My Way" to "We Did It Together."

*When we enter the new age we also turn our back on SELFISHNESS.*

Individualism says, "I did it my way!" Selfishness says, "I want it my way!"Living in community requires us to be aware of the needs, desires, and concerns of others. It requires us to practice the art of submission, to give in from time to time for the better good. It requires us to be "other" directed. Jesus said, "Love your neighbors as you love yourself" (Matthew 22:39). That is tough to do for an "I want it my way" person.

Are you familiar with property law from a toddler's perspective? It goes:

> If I like it, it's mine.
> If I can take it away from you, it's mine.
> If I had it a while ago, it's mine.
> If I say it is mine, it's mine.
> If I say I saw it first, it's mine.
> If you're having fun with it, it's mine.
> If you lay down your toy, it's mine.
> If it's broken, it's yours.[10]

Some of us have not progressed much from our toddler days. We have a ways to go in learning to put others first in a "me first" world.

One person who learned that lesson is Nick Marshall. We meet Nick (Mel Gibson) in the movie "What Women Want." He works for an advertising agency, and he is the quintessential "man's man." He's sexist. He's cocky. He thinks he is God's gift to women, and he is as self-centered as they come. He brags of his intimacy with the Swedish Bikini Team, and he is the last person one would think would ever become "other" directed.

The movie begins with Nick's looking forward to being promoted to creative director of his Chicago advertising firm. Everyone in the office assumes Nick has the promotion in his back pocket, but it does not turn out that way. Instead, Nick's boss Mr. Wannamaker (Alan Alda) gives the position to Darcy (Helen Hunt). Wannamaker says, "The eighties were our glory days. They were all about alcohol, tobacco, cars . . . Then in the nineties men simply stopped dominating how the dollars were spent . . . Women between the ages of sixteen and twenty-four are the fastest growing consumer group in the country. I love you, Nick, but it's a woman's world out there. Getting into a woman's psyche is not exactly your strong suit."

Greatly disappointed, Nick secretly vows to undermine Darcy, and a freak accident greatly aids him in the process. He falls into the bathtub with a hair dryer in his hand. He survives the electrocution, but with one major side effect: He can now hear what women think! He can read their minds, and he finds out what they really think of him. At first, he hates this new ability, but in time he sees it as a gift and begins to use it to his advantage. He literally picks Darcy's brain, beating her to every great creative idea, including her winning idea about how to market running shoes to women. He lands the big Nike account that saves the company. The boss terminates Darcy and gives the position to Nick.

Over the course of the movie, however, Nick evolves into a sensitive, caring individual. He gets in touch with his nurturing, feminine side, and comes to want what's best for others. He reaches out to a depressed co-worker, saving her life. After years of estrangement, he connects with his teenage daughter, and at the end of the movie he works to get Darcy reinstated. He tells his boss, "Dan, I had very little to do with saving the company. It's Darcy you should be thanking. If you don't get Darcy McGuire back in here, and I mean pronto, the board is going to be paying you your settlement!" He apologizes to Darcy, saying, "I took advantage of you in the worst possible way. Have you ever done that? Taken the wrong road? No, of course, you haven't. You wouldn't do that. Someone like me does that." Nick had moved from being selfish and self-centered to considerate and other-centered.

From volleyball to football, from soccer to hockey, the story is similar. Suddenly, a team clicks. It achieves greatness. It begins winning, often with the same players. The difference? Team chemistry. Legendary football coach Vince Lombardi put it well: "If you're going to play together as a team, you've got to care for one another. You've got to love each other . . . the difference between mediocrity and greatness is the feeling these guys have for each other."[11]

Teams with prima donnas—selfish, self-centered individuals—do not do as well as teams who put each other first. The same holds true for a small group. Thankfully, selfish people often refrain from joining a group, thinking to themselves, "I don't want to listen to a bunch of other people. I have better things to do with my time." If they do join, however, they will likely suck the life out of it.

*When we enter the new age, we turn our back on SELF-SUFFICIENCY.*

Individualism says, "I did it my way." Selfishness says, "I want it my way." Self-sufficiency says, "I can do it myself." If we think we can do it ourselves, we see little need of getting together with others. What could they possibly offer us? We have everything we need within ourselves to cope with adversity.

Billionaire Ted Turner recently said, "I've always identified with Jiminy Cricket, until Pinocchio became a real boy, Jiminy Cricket was his conscience." He paused for a moment then continued. "You know, I'm not looking for any big rewards. I'm not a religious person. I believe this life is all we have. I'm not doing what I'm doing to be rewarded in heaven or punished in hell. I'm doing it because I feel it's the right thing to do.

"Almost every religion talks about a savior coming. When you look in the mirror, when you're putting on your lipstick or shaving, you're looking at the savior. Nobody else is going to save you but yourself."[12]

On the one hand, I agree with Mr. Turner. We do need to take responsibility for our lives. We cannot sit around waiting for things to happen. Turner, however, goes too far. At times we do need a savior, and that savior is not us. As a great saint put it, we need to pray as if it all depended on God, and we need to work as if it all depended on us.

I like Snoopy's moment of self-realization. In the *Peanuts* cartoon strip, Snoopy stands alone thinking to himself: "There's one thing I've always been proud of, and that's the fact that I'm independent . . . "

In the next box, Charlie Brown walks by, carrying a bag in his hands. Seeing the bag, Snoopy's ears stand straight up. Charlie Brown has a bag of dog treats! Charlie Brown stops and tosses a treat into Snoopy's mouth.

The story ends with Snoopy once again standing alone. This time he says to himself, "Well, maybe I'm sort of semi-independent."[13]

We all need to be tossed a treat from time to time. We are not as self-sufficient, independent, and self-contained as we might think. We all have dependency needs and feelings. No matter how strong we are, no matter how responsible and dependable we may be, if we look clearly at ourselves, we will find a wish to be taken care of for a change. I would guess even Ted Turner feels that from time to time, even though he might not publicly admit it. When we own up to those needs, we open ourselves to the gifts others can give us. When we do not, we close ourselves off to those precious "treats" others can offer.

Jesus said, "Apart from me, you can do nothing" (John 15:5). Saint Paul would affirm that, and add, "apart from one another, you are swimming up stream as well."

## GROUP DISCUSSION AND SHARING

1.  **Getting to know one another** (20-40 *minutes*)
    Whether this is a new group or an ongoing group, take time to get to know one another a little better. Even if your group has been together for years, you may be surprised how much you will learn about one another from the following exercise. Take a couple of minutes to complete the sentences, and give each person three minutes to share their answers, adding any comments they would like to make about their responses. Complete each sentence with a different answer.

    **Who Are You?**[14]

    I am _____

    I am _____

    I am _____

    I am _____

    I am _____

2.  **Group Goals and Norms** (20-30 *minutes*)
    * What do you hope to get out of this group?
    * What do you hope to get out of this study?
    * What group norms would you like to adopt?
        ____ Begin and end on time
        ____ Confidentiality
        ____ Regular Attendance
        ____ Shared Leadership
        ____ Equalized Participation
        ____ No Advice Giving
        ____ Self-Disclosure

_____ Refreshments
_____ Adopt a Group Project
_____ Scheduled Social Gatherings
_____ Babysitting
_____ Meeting Place
_____ Other

3.    **Group Study** *(2-15 minutes)*

If group members have had a chance to read this chapter before meeting for the first time, discuss:

- What comments would you like to make about the material in this chapter?

If group members did not read the chapter before the first meeting:

- Assign Chapters 1 and 2 for next time you come together.

4.    **Sharing Prayer Concerns and Prayer** *(15-20 minutes)*

- How would you like the group to be praying for you in the days ahead?
- If this is an ongoing group, close in prayer as you would normally do. If this is a new group, be aware that group prayer, especially praying out loud, can be threatening to some. In light of that, close in silent prayer. While praying, picture the face of each individual in the group and thank God for him or her. Be still for a couple of minutes.

CHAPTER TWO

# BE DEVOTED TO ONE ANOTHER

Be devoted to one another in brotherly love.
Romans 12:10 NIV

Eugene Peterson in his fresh and provocative rendering of the New Testament, translates the above verse as, "Be good friends who love deeply."[1]

If your small group clicks on all cylinders, that is what will happen. You will become good friends, and you will come to love one another deeply. You will be like that boy whose father asked him, "If all your friends jumped off a cliff, would you jump off as well?"

The boy thought for a moment and answered, "No, if all my friends jumped off a cliff, I would be at the bottom to catch them."

What a joy it is to have friends who love us deeply. On May 26, 1953, George Bush, Sr., wrote a letter to one of his best friends, Thomas "Lud" Ashley, a classmate from Yale, shortly after learning that their three-year-old daughter, Robin, was suffering from advanced leukemia:

> Dear Lud,
> When thinking about Robin's illness, I cannot help but get philosophical—I have stopped asking "why." One thing I do know is that when one is worried or suffering or troubled that there are only two things which help, friendships and faith. I will say no more, but you have helped us both in a time of need. A few tougher days will probably lie ahead, Lud, but I don't believe many will be rougher than those first couple of weeks. We will have wonderful memories of people who helped us and tried to help us, but none will exceed in my mind your many gestures of true friendship . . . "[2]

## PAUL'S FRIENDS

At the end of his letter to the church in Colossae, the Apostle Paul introduces us to some of his friends. They compose his small group. Many of these people have been with Paul for years, and some for only a short time. And like former President Bush, what got Paul through the tough times in life were his friendships and his faith. When we ponder how Paul withstood all he withstood, when we ponder how he mustered so much courage in the face of shipwrecks, imprisonments, and beatings, it comes down to these two things: friendships and faith. Listen to what Paul says about his friends:

> *Tychicus* will tell you all the news about me; he is a beloved brother, a faithful minister, and a fellow servant in the Lord. I have sent him to you for this very purpose, so that you may know how we are and that he may encourage your hearts; he is coming with *Onesimus*, the faithful and beloved brother, who is one of you. They will tell you about everything here.
>
> *Aristarchus* my fellow prisoner greets you, as does *Mark* the cousin of *Barnabas*, concerning whom you have received instructions—if he comes to you, welcome him. And *Jesus* who is called *Justus* greets you. These are the only ones of the circumcision among my co-workers for the kingdom of God, and they have been a comfort to me. *Epaphras*, who is one of you, a servant of Jesus Christ, greets you. He is always wrestling in his prayers on your behalf, so that you may stand mature and fully assured in everything that God wills. For I testify for him that he has worked hard for you and for those in Laodicea and in Hierapolis. *Luke*, the beloved physician, and *Demas* greet you. (Colossians 4:7-14)

I won't go into great detail about all the people mentioned here, but I do want to say some things about some of them. For example, take Tychicus. Note the relationship Paul had with him. Paul calls him "a beloved brother" and says he "will tell you all the news about me." Note the intimacy between these two men. Tychicus knows Paul. He can relate all the news about him. How many people can we call a dear brother or sister in Christ? How many people can relate all the news about us?

Then there was Onesimus. I mention him because we hear of him elsewhere in the Bible in Paul's letter to Philemon. Philemon had been the master of a runaway slave named Onesimus, who had become important to Paul. Paul had written asking for Onesimus' freedom, and we can tell by the fact that Paul is now sending Onesimus as a "faithful and beloved brother" that Philemon granted Paul's request. Onesimus is a member of Paul's inner circle, his small group.

There are three other people Paul mentions that I want to highlight. One is Mark. At one point in Paul's ministry, Paul did not have any use for Mark. He told Barnabas, Mark's cousin, that he would sooner suck a lemon than take Mark on the road with him again. Barnabas, however, stuck up for his cousin, which led to an ugly scene in the Book of Acts (Acts 15:36-41) where Paul and Barnabas part company. Paul takes Silas, and Barnabas takes Mark, but now, years later, Mark is in Paul's small group. They have reconciled. At one point, Mark would have been the last person we would have guessed would wind up in Paul's inner circle, but here he is. In fact, the news about the reconciliation is so new that Paul tells the Colossians to welcome Mark when he comes, just in case they harbored ill feelings toward him because of what had happened between the two of them years ago. By saying, "welcome him," he's telling the Colossians that all is forgiven.

Another person I want to mention is Luke. Let me tell you a little secret about being in a small group. Many people believe their small group is the best small group. If you are in an ongoing group, you may think that yourself, and maybe you are in the best small group in the history of small groups, but let me tell you about Paul's group. Not only was Paul the most prolific New Testament writer, but also included in his group were two of the gospel writers, Luke and Mark. And Luke also wrote the Book of Acts. Just think. One-third of the New Testament came out of this small group! Of course, Paul feels the same way about Luke as he does the other guys in his group. He calls him "the beloved physician."

Then there was Demas. When talking about small group life, and friendships that develop in small groups, we would like to recount only success stories, but we cannot. Even though a small group can be wonderful, it can also be disappointing, and Demas illustrates the point. In a letter to Timothy, listen to what Paul says of Demas: "Do your best to come to me soon, for Demas, in love with this present world, has deserted me and gone to Thessalonica" (2 Timothy 4:9-10).

It would be great to share success story after success story, but sometimes people disappoint us, as Demas disappointed Paul. Just because we become members of a small group does not ensure deep friendships. To develop deep and lasting friendships, we need to work at it. We need to be devoted to one another.

## LEVELS OF FRIENDSHIP

Many people fail to achieve meaningful relationships because they do not have a clear understanding of the levels of friendship. One relationship expert distinguishes four levels of friendship.[3]

Level 1: ACQUAINTANCE
- Based on occasional contacts
- Freedom to ask general questions; public information

Level 2: CASUAL FRIENDSHIP
- Based on common interests, activities, concerns
- Freedom to ask specific questions; opinions, ideas, wishes and goals

Level 3: CLOSE FRIENDSHIP AND FELLOWSHIP
- Based on mutual life goals
- Freedom to suggest mutual projects toward reaching life goals.

Level 4: INTIMATE FRIENDSHIP AND FELLOWSHIP
- Based on commitment to the development of each other's character
- Freedom to correct each other

Level 3 and 4 friendships are not found, they are built. The quality of the effort determines the quality of the friendship. It takes commitment, vulnerability, history, and mercy.

## BUILDING FRIENDSHIPS

*One of the most basic factors in building friendships is COMMITMENT.*

Commitment was one of the secrets to Mitch Albom's and Morrie Schwartz's friendship, celebrated in the book *Tuesdays with Morrie.* Mitch and Morrie referred to themselves as "Tuesday People."[4] They first met at Brandeis University on a Tuesday. Morrie's office hours were on Tuesday afternoon, and Mitch was one of his students. Morrie became Mitch's mentor, and when Mitch renewed his relationship with Morrie, they met each Tuesday afternoon. At the end of one of their visits, Mitch leaned over to give Morrie a hug. Then he did something out of character. He kissed Morrie on the cheek. Morrie reached up with his weakened hands, and Mitch felt the thin stubble of his whiskers brushing his face. Morrie whispered in his ear, "So, you'll come back next Tuesday?"

I suppose I could write a book titled "Mondays with Hank." Hank and I attended the same church and ended up attending the same small group. Noticing my discouragement as a young pastor, Hank suggested we get together for lunch the following Monday. We have been meeting together on Mondays since 1976, whenever the two of us are both in town. We eat lunch, talk sports, review movies, and ask each other, "How can I be praying for you this week?" Hank is a "Level 4" friend. Our commitment to be together every Monday has helped us reach that level.

We will never become close to the people in our small group without making the group a high priority. It makes sense. The more time we spend together, the more we get to know one another. I feel loved when people knock themselves out to come to group. On the other hand, I do not feel very high on someone's priority list when they attend sporadically, or when the most minor "excuse" keeps them from coming. If we are content with Level 1 and 2 relationships with the people in our group, then we do not need to make the group a high priority. We can come when it suits us. However, if we want to go deeper, if we want to develop close and intimate friendships, we need to do everything we can to regularly attend group meetings.

Plato, the ancient Greek philosopher, talked a great deal about establishing our life's priorities. In one of his writings, he asks us to imagine life as a big triangle. Then he tells us to arrange, along the base of that triangle, all the things in life we regard as important. Then he tells us to start moving up the triangle toward the apex. As we proceed upward, the base will get smaller, so we will need to dispose of more and more things. We will drop things of lesser importance. Finally, when we reach the top of the triangle, the apex, there is room for one thing only.[5]

I am not suggesting that we put our friends in our small group at the very top of our triangle. Our relationship with Christ occupies that place. I am suggesting, however, that being devoted to one another requires keeping our brothers and sisters in Christ as near the top of the triangle as possible.

*Building deep and intimate friendships also requires VULNERABILITY.*

Mark Twain counseled, "Don't complain and talk about all your problems—80 percent of people don't care; the other 20 percent will think you deserve them."[6] My experience is almost the opposite of Twain's. Granted, some people can weigh us down with the burdens they bear. They feel sorry for themselves, and could care less about what troubles us. Most people, however, are not like that. Most folk just want someone to listen to them, and in talking it out, they feel better equipped to handle what is troubling them. They do not want advice; they simply want a listening ear. When people trust me with the painful and troubling aspects of their lives, I feel as if I am walking on holy ground. I do not think less of them when they confess a failure or a struggle. I actually think more of them because most people do not have the courage to share such things with another.

In his book *Bottom Line Faith*, Larry Kreider lists ten qualifications for a mentor. I find qualification four quite interesting. He writes:

> If you spend time bragging about your accomplishments and attempt to make every conversation a teachable moment, soon you'll be talking to yourself. Nothing worthwhile in life is obtained without a struggle. One of the greatest lessons you can learn is how to persevere through adversity. To teach about adversity means admitting your times of weakness. How have you overcome the jaws of fear or at times dealt with the demons of self-doubt? Admitting your weakness will take the pressure off your protégée to imitate a saint.[7]

The same can be said about friendships. If we refrain from sharing our doubts and struggles, people will go to those who do share such things.

I struggle with depression. For years I kept it a secret. I thought pastors were not supposed to get depressed; after all, joy happens to be a fruit of the Spirit (Galatians 5: 22). Each spring after Easter and each fall before stewardship, I would get depressed. One day I shared this with my associate, and that led to a citywide speaking engagement. Stetson University and Florida Hospital were planning a day-long seminar in Orlando, Florida, on depression. A Stetson psychology professor was to speak, a psychiatrist from Florida Hospital was to speak, and they wanted someone to talk about a personal experience. They especially wanted someone who was successful professionally to share his or her story. Somehow, I agreed to be a presenter. It was a watershed moment for me. I learned about different kinds of depression. I learned about different ways to treat it. I learned about helpful responses and non-helpful responses to a depressed person, and most importantly, what I might do with mine. I decided to go on medication to balance the chemical imbalance within my body. I had been fighting that decision for years. What a remarkable difference that has made! I now understand, for the first time, what it feels like to be normal, and not get stuck in a whirlpool of hopelessness. I still get "blue" from time to time, but not depressed.

For years, I feared that if people knew about my depression, they would steer clear of me. I thought my parishioners would think less of me. The opposite happened. People with depression, people with depressed friends, people with depressed family members all came in to see me. They wanted counsel. They wanted to know what could be done about it. Instead of driving people away, my vulnerability drew people to me. I was human, not a saint.

A physician named John offered a revealing example of what vulnerable self-disclosure can do in a group. He said,

> Someone shared about their struggles with their marriage and how they . . . had struggled soon after they were married with their . . . relationship and that kind of thing. What that does is give permission . . . When people expose areas of brokenness in their lives, it gives you much more legitimacy to expose your areas of brokenness. And so when that happened, suddenly we found all the fractured couples in the group. Had that not happened, I think that we still wouldn't know about those fractured relationships that we want to encourage and help.[8]

One definition of friendship reads, "Friendship is the comfort of feeling safe with a person and needing not to weigh one's thoughts or to measure one's words." John began developing that kind of friendship with the people in his small group. If we are going to devote ourselves to one another, like John, we need to risk being vulnerable with one another. It's the path we need to take to develop Level 3 and Level 4 friendships.

*Building friendships also requires HISTORY.*

George Washington said, "Be courteous to all, but intimate with few, and let those few be well tried before you give them your confidence. True friendship is a plant of slow growth, and must undergo and withstand the shocks of adversity before it is entitled to the appellation.[9]

A long-time friend had what my wife calls a "mental-hormone day." It was a few days before Christmas and everything looked bleak to her. Old wounds of rejection opened once again. Her self-esteem registered "empty" on her emotional tank. We had intended to have lunch together, but she was not up to going. She called me and said, "I need to cancel lunch. I'm having one of those days. Can we make it another time."

I said, "Sure," and then added, "Do you need to talk to someone?"

She replied, "Yes, would you come by?"

I went by and listened as she talked. After an hour, I left and told her I would call later to see how she was doing. The next morning she e-mailed me these words:

> A simple friend has never seen you cry.
> A real friend has shoulders soggy from your tears.
>
> A simple friend doesn't know your parent's first names.
> A real friend has their phone numbers in his address book.
>
> A simple friend seeks to talk with you about their problems.
> A real friend seeks to help you with your problems.
>
> A simple friend, when visiting, acts like a guest.
> A real friend opens your refrigerator and helps themselves.

A simple friend thinks the relationship is over
    when you have an argument.
A real friend knows that it's not a friendship
    until after you've had a fight.

A simple friend expects you to always be there for them.
A real friend expects to always be there for you!

My best friendships have stood the test of time. They have weathered storms of adversity. They have survived misunderstandings, disappointments, and arguments. They have become like Charlie and Martha Shedd's relationship. Charlie and Martha loved each other dearly. They traveled the country speaking on marriage and parenting. Charlie, a prolific writer, wrote some great books, my favorites being *Letters to Philip, Letters to Karen*, and *The Stork is Dead*. In one of their seminars, they spoke about the importance of affirming love for one another, no matter how difficult it might be at the time. To illustrate their point, Martha told of a time she was hopping mad at Charlie. Martha got so mad that her anger stayed with her through the night. After awaking the next morning, she decided she needed to go for a walk in order to blow off a little steam. Charlie was still in bed, so Martha left him a note on the kitchen table. She wrote,

Dear Charlie,

I have gone for a walk.
I hate you.

Love,
Martha

My best friendships feel like that. We may disappoint one another. We may see things differently, and we may even tick one another off, but we still love one another. I know those friends will not leave me, or I them. We have made it through tough times. We will make it through additional tough times. We do not doubt our devotion to one another. Our relationship has been time-tested.

*Finally, building deep friendships calls for liberal doses of MERCY.*
    There was a young man in Napoleon's army who committed a deed so terrible that it was worthy of death. The day before he was

scheduled for the firing squad, the young man's mother went to Napoleon and pleaded for mercy for her son.

Napoleon replied, "Woman, your son does not deserve mercy."

"I know," she answered. "If he deserved it, then it would not be mercy."

Many a time I have failed as a friend. I have been insensitive, shortsighted, stubborn, and neglectful. My best friends, however, have not held that against me. When I least deserved it, they extended mercy to me.

Jesus said, "Blessed are the merciful, for they will receive mercy" (Matthew 5:7). And they also will have a number of friends. Lloyd Ogilvie, Chaplain of the United States Senate, asks,

> If you had to choose one word to describe the nature of God, what word would you choose? All-powerful? All-knowing? Forgiving? Gracious?
>
> My word would be *merciful*. Whatever other words I might use are all part of this magnificent quality of mercy. I'm not alone in my choice. In the Old Testament alone, the word is used nearly two hundred times to describe the nature of God.[10]

Abba Arika, a celebrated sage who died in 247, asked, "When God prays, how would he pray?" He suggested, "May it be my will that my mercy may suppress my anger, that my mercy may prevail over my other attributes, so that I may deal with my children in the attribute of mercy and on their behalf stop short of the limit of stern justice."[11]

If I had to choose one word to describe the nature of an intimate friend, I would chose "merciful" as well. A child said to his mother, "My teacher thinks I'm going to be famous. She said all I have to do is mess up one more time and I'm history." Level 4 friends do not tell us we are history. Level 4 friends know our flaws, have experienced our flaws, at times have become frustrated with our flaws, and love us still. I think of Trudy and Brenda. They are as close as friends can be. They meet regularly, but every now and again—not often, but every now and again—Trudy gets wrapped up into something and misses a meeting. When Trudy realizes her error, she feels awful, and she apologizes profusely. Brenda gets upset, but Brenda always extends mercy. Mercy holds the relationship together.

## A QUIZ

There is a popular quiz that is worth taking:

*Name the ten wealthiest people in the world.*
*Name the last ten Heisman trophy winners.*
*Name the last ten winners of the Miss America contest.*
*Name eight people who have won the Nobel or Pulitzer Prize.*
*How about the last ten Academy Award winners for best picture*
*    or the last decade's worth of World Series winners?*

How did you do? I didn't do well either. With the exception of you trivia hounds, none of us remember the headliners of yesterday too well. Surprising how quickly we forget, isn't it? And what I've mentioned above are no second-rate achievements. Awards tarnish. Achievements are forgotten. Accolades and certificates are buried with their owners.

Here's the other half of the quiz. See how you do on this part:

*Think of three people you enjoy spending time with.*
*Name ten people who have taught you something worthwhile.*
*Name five friends who have helped you in a difficult time.*
*List a few teachers who have aided your journey through school.*
*Name a half-dozen heroes whose stories have inspired you.*

Easier? It was for me, too. The lesson? The people who make a difference are not the ones with the credentials, but the ones with the concern. Enjoy life and remember the important things . . . your friends along your path through life.

## GROUP DISCUSSION AND SHARING

1.  **Icebreaker** *(20-30 minutes)*
    - This past week I devoted myself to ...
    - Something I wish I had devoted myself to ...

2.  **Discussion** *(20-35 minutes)*
    If you did not discuss chapter one from your last time together, what comments would you like to make about it?

- What struck you about the Apostle Paul's small group?
- What other building blocks of friendship would you add to the four (commitment, vulnerability, history, mercy) mentioned in the chapter?
- What might "being devoted to one another" look like in your small group?

3.  **Sharing** *(20-30 minutes)*
    - To what do you want to devote yourself this coming week?
    - How can the group be praying for you?

4.  **Praying** *(5-10 minutes)*
    Close in your normal manner, or do a "popcorn" prayer. In "popcorn" prayer, only words or short phrases are spoken. The leader divides the time into two sections: thanksgiving and intercession (praying for others). The leader begins by saying, "God, we give thanks for . . . " and group members utter a word or short phrase that captures their sense of thanksgiving, such as "health," "new friends," "time to slow down," and so on. Members utter words and phrases as they pop into their mind. There is no going around a circle. Some may utter a number of words or phrases, while others may remain silent. After a couple of minutes of thanksgiving, the leader says, "And now, God, we bring before you these concerns . . . " and again words or short phrases are uttered, such as "Martha's job interview," "the election," "Jim's daughter," and so on. After a couple of minutes of intercession, the leader simply closes by saying, "God, thank you for hearing our prayers. Amen."

CHAPTER THREE

# SPEAK TRUTHFULLY WITH ONE ANOTHER

So then, putting away all falsehood let all of us speak the truth to our neighbors, for we are members of one another.
Ephesians 4:25

Do not lie to one another, seeing that you have stripped off the old self with its practices.
Colossians 3:9

A pastor told her congregation, "Next week I plan to preach about the sin of lying. To help you understand my sermon, I want all of you to read Mark 17."

The following Sunday, as she prepared to deliver her sermon, the pastor asked for a show of hands. She wanted to know how many had read Mark 17. Every hand went up. The pastor smiled and said, "Mark has only sixteen chapters. I will now proceed with my sermon on lying."

\* \* \*

A fisherman arrived at the Pearly Gates of Heaven. Peter asked him what he wanted. The fisherman said, "I want to come in."

"You can't come in here," Peter replied. "You've told too many lies."

"Have a heart, Peter," said the man. "After all, you were a fisherman once yourself."

\* \* \*

A preacher saw a group of young boys sitting in a circle with a dog in the middle. He asked them what they were doing with the dog. One little fellow said, "We ain't doin' nuthin' to the dog. We're just telling lies, and the one that tells the biggest one gets to keep the dog."

The preacher told them that when he was a little boy, he never would have even thought of telling a lie.

The little boy said, "Give him the dog, fellas."

* * *

Finally, Leonard Sweet in his *Soul Café* newsletter, included his list of "Top 10 Liars' Lies":

10. We'll stay only five minutes.
9. This will be a short meeting.
8. I'll respect you in the morning.
7. The check is in the mail.
6. I'm from the government, and I'm here to help you.
5. This hurts me more than it hurts you.
4. Your money will be cheerfully refunded.
3. We service what we sell.
2. Your table will be ready in just a minute.
1. I'll start exercising (dieting, forgiving, . . . ) tomorrow.

* * *

In the ninth commandment, God bans lying: "You shall not bear false witness against your neighbor" (Exodus 20:16). Apparently, not everyone knows about the ban. A house committee estimated that one out of every three working Americans with educational or career credentials have altered those credentials on their resumes. The State of Wisconsin discovered that forty-seven percent of students would cheat on an exam, and sixty-six percent said they would lie to achieve a business objective. A CNN poll suggests that seven out of ten people are dissatisfied with current standards of honesty, and some don't even call them lies anymore. They call them "strategic misrepresentations," or "reality augmentations," or "terminological exactitudes."

We have become a nation of truth-fudgers and honesty-dodgers. Let me mention the most common types of lies.

## EIGHT COMMON LIES[1]

*First, there are LIES FOR PROFIT.* Some lie to make a buck.

At a birthday party, it came time to serve the cake. A little boy named Brian blurted out, "I want the biggest piece!"

His mother quickly scolded him. "Brian, it's not polite to ask for the biggest piece."

The little guy looked at her in confusion, and asked, "Well, then, how do you get it?"

Some attempt to get the biggest piece of the financial cake by lying.

I was shocked. I still cannot believe what happened. I was in the market for a new car. We had just moved back to Omaha, Nebraska, from Orlando, Florida, and I wanted a four-wheel drive vehicle. I knew my Mazda Miata would not navigate well in the snow. I needed something more rugged, something more solid. I scanned the ads one Saturday morning and came across a sure come-on. The new models had just come out, and a dealership advertised a great sale on last year's Jeep Cherokees. The dealership only had six left, and they were discounting them by $3,000. They also were offering 1.9% financing. I went to the dealership knowing there would be a catch. Surely, they would claim to have sold the cars the night before the ads hit the paper, or surely the financing would not really be 1.9%. It would be higher because you needed to be a first-time buyer to get that rate, or some other reason. But that was not the case. When I arrived on the lot, they had one Jeep Cherokee left. The salesman said if I liked the color, I could purchase it with a $3,000 discount and at 1.9% financing. I bought it on the spot. I could not believe it. There was no catch. They were not lying to make a buck.

Unfortunately, some do. Used-car salespeople, televangelists, and cigarette companies have been known to stretch the truth to line their pockets.

*Second, there are LIES OF BOASTING.*

We tell lies in order to impress others. Very few people, for instance, can resist the temptation to tell a story in such a way that puts them in a better light than the facts warrant. Even the best of us relate what we would like to have said and done in a particular situation rather than what we actually did say and do. Not only that, but we also drop names and call people we barely know "friends." Pastors can be particularly guilty of the lie of boasting. At a conference someone might ask, "How many people worship with you on a weekly basis?" and most pastors fudge a little bit by factoring in their Easter and Christmas attendance to pad the statistics. As someone said, "I'm not a liar, sir. I just remember big!"

*Third, there are LIES OF MALICE.*

Someone hurts us, or we are jealous of someone's success, so we concoct a story or a rumor to get back at the other person. I recall reading an article a number of years ago about the Hall of Fame quarterback, Joe Montana. When Joe was the quarterback of the San Francisco 49ers (he finished his career with the Kansas City Chiefs), some people, jealous of his success, told lies about him, saying he had a drug habit. When Joe watched television that night and saw the story on national TV, he began to weep because he loved kids and did not want to set a poor example.

In politics they are called "dirty tricks." You spread falsehoods about opponents to undermine their credibility and elect-ability. Whatever we call it—dirty tricks, gossip, backbiting, slander—God condemns it. A sage in the Old Testament wrote, "A perverse person spreads strife, and a whisperer separates close friends" (Proverbs 16:28). The Apostle Paul said, "Put away from you all bitterness and wrath and anger and wrangling and slander, together with all malice" (Ephesians 4:31).

*Fourth, there are LIES OF FEAR.*

We tell a lie to escape punishment. It begins in childhood when we realize our parents are not omniscient. We tell them we did not take such and such or push so and so, and they believe us. They take us at our word, and we get off without a dire consequence. From that moment on, we learn that if we bend the truth or deny it, we might escape retribution or a reprimand.

I recall that moment when I looked my mother in the eye and told a bold-faced lie. My best friend and I needed money to buy a model airplane. To get money, I often returned bottles for refunds, or I searched the cushions of the couch or chair for stray coins. This particular time, however, there were no bottles to return and no money had slipped under a cushion from a pant pocket. So, I sneaked into my mother's purse and took two dollars. Later she asked me if I had been in her purse. I told her, "No, why do you ask?" She said, "I thought I had more money in my wallet than I have now."

I got the model, but I felt awful. It was the one and only time I took money from my mother's purse.

*Fifth, there are LIES TO PLEASE PEOPLE.*

We tell a lie to keep others happy. Wetherall Johnson, founder of Bible Study Fellowship, gives an account of such an experience when she was a missionary in China. She pretended to like something when she really did not like it at all. She wanted to make her host happy.

> A wonderful meal was set out for us on a small table under the trees. The food was covered by big blue flies, which the Chinese kept swatting away. Finally, we sat down in Chinese fashion, with the wife of the host serving us. We were just three missionaries with the Chinese host, who was the only man. By this time we were well used to chopsticks, rice, sweet and sour pork, and fish. At this table there was a huge codfish complete with head and big eyes.
>
> We were able to enjoy the conversation. For some unknown reason, I happened to be seated next to the host. Suddenly, he used his own chopsticks to place in my bowl of rice the greatest delicacy of the feast; namely, one of the cod's huge eyes! He smiled, thinking how honored I would feel. Honored! Looking longingly at the chickens feeding underneath the table, I smiled at my host and I looked at Miss McQueen and knew what I had to do. I thanked God I possessed a large throat—one swallow and it was over. Never again did I have such a "treat," for this delicacy belonged to that region only! A true missionary always eats what is put before her like the Chinese; she is supposed to "become Chinese." God helped me to keep down that ugly cod's eye.[2]

I do something similar with my wife, Trudy. I fudge the truth. I am less than honest in order to make her feel good about herself. The other day she asked, "Does my hair style make my head look big?" She followed that up with, "That's a dumb question. There is no way you are going to say 'yes' to that!" She hit the nail on the head. When Trudy asks, "Does this dress make me look fat?" or "Does this color wash me out?" I will often ask her, "What's the right answer?" To say one's spouse looks less than stunning can lead to disaster, so at times I fudge the truth to keep a smile on Trudy's face.

*Sixth, there are LIES OF SILENCE.*

Sometimes the easiest way to avoid trouble is to do or say nothing. We find ourselves agreeing with bosses or teachers or leaders because we do not want to upset the apple cart. In private we kick ourselves and say, "I should not have agreed with her. I should not have bought into what she was saying. I just shook my head and said, 'Yes.' I should have said what I really thought."

By remaining silent we may indicate support for something we know to be wrong. Robert Louis Stevenson lived a mere forty-four years, but he said some wonderful things in that short span of time:[3] "Old and young, we are all on our last cruise." "Mankind was never so happily inspired as when it made a cathedral." "The cruelest lies are often told in silence." Silence is not always golden.

The biblical commentator William Barclay points out that one of the more interesting facts about the Jewish law is that the one who refuses to give evidence, when he or she has evidence to give, is condemned as severely as the one who gives false evidence.[4] He directs us to Leviticus 5:1: "When any of you sin in that you have heard a public adjuration to testify and—though able to testify as one who has seen or learned of the matter—does not speak up, you are subject to punishment." In other words, according to the Bible, a cowardly or careless or irresponsible silence can be as serious a crime as false and lying speech. One can sin through speech *and* through silence.

*Seventh, there are LIES OF EXAGGERATION.*

A wife says to her husband, "You *never* listen to me." A husband says to a wife, "You are *always* late." Is that true? Does the husband never listen to his wife? Is the wife always late? Doubtful. These are lies of exaggeration, and they undermine constructive communication by polarizing a relationship.

Then there are those lies of exaggeration we tell ourselves. We say things to ourselves like, "If I tell my boss what's happening, he will kill me!" Really? Will the boss take out a gun and shoot us? Not likely. Or we say to ourselves, "If that happens to me, I'll just die." Really? Keel over dead? That is an exaggeration. We may get embarrassed. We may become humiliated. We may become uncomfortable, but keel over dead? Doubtful. The trouble with these private lies is that they debilitate us. They paralyze our inner being because we start believing these outrageous exaggerations that float around in our minds, which results in timid, anxious, and fearful behavior.

When I preached every Sunday, I often told one of these types of lies. I cannot count the number of times on a Sunday night when I turned to Trudy and said, "Well, that's the last sermon I'll ever preach. I'll never be able to come up with something by next Sunday." That lie resulted in my being on pins and needles until I got the sermon written for the next Sunday. I was a bear to be around on Mondays and Tuesdays, my primary sermon writing days.

*Eighth, there are LIES OF CONVENIENCE.*

Parents lie, writing "sick" notes for their children at school when they were not sick. Secretaries lie when they answer the phone and say, "The boss isn't in," when she is. We make up an erroneous excuse for why we weren't at a particular function because it's easier to explain our absence with a lie.

Dr. Paul Brand tells the story of a female patient who had come to see him. After diagnosing her with gastritis, the woman's eyes filled with tears. He attempted to tell her it was nothing serious, and easily treatable, but she did not believe him. He soon found out why the diagnosis shook her so:

> She then told me the story about her mother, who had suffered a long, painful disease. "One tortuous night the family doctor made a house call while mother was groaning and pressing her hands to her stomach. She was feverish and obviously suffering. When the doctor arrived, mother said, 'Doctor, am I really going to get better? I feel so ill and have lost so much weight . . . I think I must be dying.'
>
> "The doctor put his hand on my mother's shoulder, looked at her with a tender expression, and replied, 'I know how you feel. It hurts badly, doesn't it? But we can lick this one—it is simply gastritis. If you take this medicine for a little while longer, with these tranquilizers, we will have you on your feet in no time. You'll feel better before you know it. Don't worry. Just trust me.' My mother smiled and thanked him. I was overwhelmed by the doctor's kindness.

"In the hallway, out of her hearing, the doctor turned to me and said gravely, 'I'm afraid your mother will not last more than a day or two. She has an advanced case of cancer of the stomach. If we keep her tranquilized, she will probably pass away peacefully. If there's anyone you should notify . . . '

"I interrupted him in mid-sentence. 'But, doctor! You told her she was doing fine!'"

Dr. Paul Brand reflected on his patient's story about the less-than-truthful doctor, and he came to the following conclusion:

Occasions will come when to be untruthful is more convenient or less offensive. But a respect for truth cannot be worn and then casually removed like a jacket; it cannot be contracted and then relaxed like a muscle. Either it is rigid and dependable, like healthy bone, or it is useless.[5]

## THE IMPACT OF LYING

Ever wonder why God prohibited lying in the Ten Commandments? That is to say, ever wonder why a prohibition against lying made God's top ten? On a similar note, ever wonder why the Apostle Paul made such a big thing about lying and truth telling in his letters to the Colossians and Ephesians? Ever wonder why he said, "Do not lie to one another," and why he said, "So then, putting away falsehood, let all of us speak the truth to our neighbors"? I can only venture a guess, but three possibilities come to mind.

One reason has to do with what lying does to relationships. Simply put, lying damages relationships, often irreparably. We hate when someone lies to us. We can withstand a misunderstanding. We can overlook a miscommunication, but an outright deception, a bold-faced lie, shakes the foundation of a friendship. We wonder if we can ever trust the person again.

As a parent, I could overlook a number of things. I could overlook a dirty room. I could overlook spilled milk at the table. I could overlook moody behavior. But I could not overlook a lie. If I ever caught our children in a lie, the consequences were much more severe than if they had simply admitted whatever they had tried to cover-up by lying. Lying is serious business. Of course, I am not alone in this. One of the six things God abhors is "a false witness who breathes out lies" (Proverbs 6:19).

That leads us to the second reason for the prohibition on lying. We are to tell the truth because lying gives God the "heebie jeebies." Let me see if I can explain. My daughter plays the piano, and I've noticed something over the years about Jenny and her playing: It drives Jenny batty when the piano is out of tune. I seldom notice an out-of-tune piano, but Jenny has a very sensitive ear. She has a great sense of pitch, and if the piano is out of tune, if the notes are not true, she hears it immediately and she almost physically shakes when she hears it. Someone filing their fingernails or scratching their nails on a chalkboard does that to me, but an out-of-tune piano does it to her. When a note is not true, it sends shivers up her spine, and something similar happens to God. Listen to these words: "There are six things that the Lord hates, seven that are an abomination to him: haughty eyes, a lying tongue, and hands that shed innocent blood, a heart that devises wicked plans, feet that hurry to run to evil, a lying witness who testifies falsely, and one who sows discord in a family" (Proverbs 6:16-19). Of the seven things that God hates, two have to do with lying: God detests a lying tongue and a false witness who pours out lies.

Why? God detests it because God is truth. Jesus said, "I am the way, and the truth, and the life" (John 14:6). God is absolute truth, and when a person lies, it goes against everything God represents. It runs cross current to who God is. Not only that, a lie sends a chill up God's spine because God knows that it was a lie that got humankind in trouble in the first place. Remember Satan saying to Eve, "If you eat of this forbidden fruit, you shall not die. God said you would die, but you won't die. God doesn't want you to enjoy the world God has created. God is a big cosmic killjoy. Go ahead and eat the fruit. Enjoy life." Remember that lie? The suffering, the pain, the mistreatment experienced around the world can be traced back to that lie. A lie opened the floodgates of evil in the world.

Finally, lying is to be avoided because of the adverse affect it will have on building authentic community in a small group. Listen to these words from M. Scott Peck:

> On my lecture tours across the country the one constant I have found wherever I go—the Northeast, the Southeast, the Midwest, Southwest, or West Coast—is the lack—and the thirst for—community.

This lack and thirst is particularly heartbreaking in those places where one might expect to find real community: in churches . . .

In our culture of rugged individualism—in which we generally feel that we dare not be honest about ourselves, even with the person in the pew next to us—we bandy around the word "community." We apply it to almost any collection of individuals—a town, a church, a synagogue, a fraternal organization, an apartment complex, a professional association—regardless of how poorly those individuals communicate with each other. It is a false use of the word.

If we are going to use the word meaningfully we must restrict it to a group of individuals who have learned how to communicate honestly with each other, whose relationships go deeper than their masks of composure, and have developed some significant commitment to "rejoice together, mourn together," and to "delight in each other, make others' conditions our own."[6]

If we are less than honest with one another, if we cover up our "real selves," we will experience what Peck calls "pseudo-community." We will not experience the real thing. Being honest with one another means telling the truth about ourselves: our needs, our fears, our frustrations, our hopes, and our dreams.

Pastor and author John Claypool tells of the time he received an invitation to be in a small group. After joining the group, he made the following observation,

We were all so much more alike than I had realized. Then, too, I was amazed to see that in that context honesty evoked compassion. Whenever a person was authentic enough to take off his mask and let his true condition be seen, instead of being condemned or exploited, I found all kinds of insight and concern flowed to him as a response.[7]

That has been my experience as well. I have been in a small group with a number of great people, but one of my favorites has been Dave Wallace. Dave is in his early eighties now. He is a recovering alcoholic and has had an interesting spiritual journey. He has been in and out of Catholic, Unitarian, and Presbyterian churches. The other day he admitted to our small group that he never joined any of those churches because he was not a person of faith. He said, "I'm trying, but I have difficulty believing. I am on a spiritual quest, and I hope some day to find my way, but I cannot speak of faith in the same way you speak of faith. I hope that is okay. It scares me a little to tell you this." Of course, it was okay with us. Dave's willingness over the years to share about his alcoholism, his fears, and his screw-ups has endeared us to him. If Dave had lied about himself, if he had been less than honest with us, we would not have loved him as much as we do now. Dave's truthful sharing has helped us be more honest about ourselves, and though it may surprise him, we look upon him as a man with considerable faith.

## A THORNY QUESTION

Before I close these reflections on lying, one question raises its thorny head: Is it ever permissible to lie? Are all white lies necessarily bad? Does not social etiquette encourage us to refrain from brutal honesty from time to time? When invited to a party we do not want to attend, isn't it better to say, "I am already engaged on the 20th" than to say, "Thanks, but I don't want to come"? Must we say to the pastor on the way out of the sanctuary, "Your sermon today was boring and trite"? When meeting someone at a movie or a restaurant, should we tell the truth? Should we say, "You look awful in that outfit!" or is it acceptable not to say a thing?

Was Martin Luther correct when he wrote a friend and said, "What harm would it do if a man told a good strong lie for the sake of the good and for the Christian Church? . . . a useful lie, a helpful lie. Such lies would not be against God; he would accept them."[8]

Is there such a thing as helpful, useful lies? For example, do evil people deserve the truth? When the Gestapo arrived at the door, was it wrong for those hiding Jews to withhold the truth? Moreover, is it permissible to withhold the truth to protect those we love? Is it wrong for a wife to lie to her husband about her promiscuous past knowing full well such knowledge might end the marriage? Should parents tell their children that they used drugs when they were in college? Are there some things better left unsaid?

Is it ever permissible to lie? I leave that discussion to your group. Let me only say that the Scriptures remind us that we need to have a bias toward truthfulness in every situation we encounter. To tell a lie places a burden of proof on us. Before telling a lie we need to ask, "Is it useful? Is it justified? Will it advance the Kingdom of God?"

## GROUP DISCUSSION AND SHARING

1. **Icebreaker** *(20-30 minutes)*
   - Speaking the truth in love, share a high point and a low point from your past week.
   - Name a time you lied or a time someone lied to you.

2. **Discussion** *(20-30 minutes)*
   - Do you believe we ought to be honest with each other in the group, revealing warts and all?
   - Is it ever justified to tell a lie? Under what circumstances? How does that impact your understanding of the ninth commandment?
   - What additional remarks would you like to make about the chapter?

3. **Sharing** *(15-30 minutes)*
   - Which of the eight common types of lies come most readily to you? Choose one or two. Which do not seem to be much of a problem for you? Again, choose one or two.
     - ____ Lies for profit
     - ____ Lies of boasting
     - ____ Lies of malice
     - ____ Lies of fear
     - ____ Lies to please people
     - ____ Lies of silence
     - ____ Lies of exaggeration
     - ____ Lies of convenience
   - How can the group be praying for you this coming week?

4.   **Praying** *(5-10 minutes)*
Close in your normal manner or pray silently for each member of
the group. The leader will mention each person by name. As each
person is mentioned, pray silently for that person for twenty to
thirty seconds. After each person has been upheld in silent
prayer, close by praying The Lord's Prayer as a group.

CHAPTER FOUR

# DO NOT GRUMBLE AGAINST ONE ANOTHER

Beloved, do not grumble against one another, so that you
may not be judged. See, the Judge is standing at the doors!
James 5:9

A middle-aged man, famous for his constant complaining, and a
nuisance to everyone who knew him, inherited a lot of money. After observing that it wasn't as much as he thought it should be, he told
his wife, a gentle-spirited woman, that he thought he would buy some
acreage for them to enjoy in their retirement. "What do you think I
should name my spread?" he asked. She replied, "Why don't you call it
"Belly Acres?"

Moses certainly had his share of "belly-acres." Bellyache number one came on the way out of Egypt. The Israelites appeared to be in
deep weeds. Pharaoh's elite army was closing fast, and the recently liberated Israelites had no earthly means of escape. Terrified, they cried
out to the Lord, and then said to Moses,

> Was it because there were no graves in Egypt that you
> have taken us away to die in the wilderness? What have
> you done to us, bringing us out of Egypt? Is this not the
> very thing we told you in Egypt, 'Let us alone and let us
> serve the Egyptians'? For it would have been better for
> us to serve the Egyptians than to die in the wilderness.
> (Exodus 14:11-12)

You know the rest of the story. Moses told them to have faith
and stand firm because everything was under control. There was nothing to fear because the Lord would fight for them. And God did. God
parted the sea and the Israelites walked to safety. Of course, I like the
way one nine-year-old boy told it. Bursting out of Sunday School, he

could hardly wait to tell his parents what he had learned that morning. After locating his father, he said, "Dad, that story of Moses and all those people crossing the Red Sea was great!" His father smiled and asked his son to tell him about it.

"Well, the Israelites got out of Egypt, but Pharaoh and his army chased after them. So the Jews ran as fast as they could until they got to the Red Sea. The Egyptian Army was getting closer and closer. So Moses got on his walkie-talkie and told the Israeli Air Force to bomb the Egyptians. While that was happening, the Israeli Navy built a pontoon bridge so the people could cross over. They made it!"

By now the father was shocked. "Is that the way they taught you the story?"

"Well, no, not exactly," said the boy, "but if I told it to you the way they told it to us, you'd never believe it, Dad."

We can certainly appreciate why Moses' people were complaining. The ways of God were new to them. After five-hundred years of bondage, they had little experience with the God of Abraham, Isaac, and Jacob. Furthermore, the situation looked bad. They did not have a lot of history with Moses, and his idea to camp where they did—on the banks of the sea—seemed to have been a tactical mistake. Little did they know that God had instructed Moses to camp there. God wanted no doubt in anyone's mind—Egyptian or Israeli—about who rescued the Israelites. There was no earthly means of escape, but there was a heavenly one. After God rescued them, it seems impossible that they would have doubts about God's power and Moses' leadership.

That, however, was not the case. One would have thought that the parting of the Red Sea would have sealed the deal for the Israelites. One would have thought that God's power and Moses' leadership were no longer in question. Not true! Three days later, they were bellyaching once again—this time about the lack of water.

When the Israelites left Egypt, they carried out unleavened bread, and probably great quantities of water. Water, of course, is heavy (about sixty-two pounds per cubic foot), and humans use it in greater quantities than food. So, it would be no surprise that, as they crossed the wilderness, they ran out of water before running out of food. Stumbling upon their first watering hole, and finding it brackish, they became frustrated and uttered bellyache number two: We are going to die of thirst!

> Then Moses ordered Israel to set out from the Red Sea,
> and they went into the wilderness of Shur. They went

three days in the wilderness and found no water. When they came to Marah, they could not drink the water of Marah because it was bitter. And the people complained against Moses, saying, "What shall we drink?" He cried out to the Lord; and the Lord showed him a piece of wood; he threw it into the water, and the water became sweet. (Exodus 15:22-25)

Not only did the water become sweet, and not only did they drink to their hearts' desire, but also Moses led them to a natural oasis fed by twelve springs of water and shaded by seventy palm trees! Surely, the Israelites would get it now. Surely, the Israelites would be certain of God's providential care. God had not only delivered them from the Egyptians, but also from thirst and dehydration. Surely, there was nothing to fear. Surely, there was much to celebrate. Surely, life was sweet.

Yes, it was, but not for long. The Israelites faced a third crisis. They had escaped the Egyptians. They had quenched their thirst. Now they were hungry. They had run out of food. That was not surprising. Travelers figure on forty days of food when they set across the Sinai Peninsula. The Israelites have already been on the road for more than a month. So what do they do? Pray? Ask God to provide? Not quite. They bellyache once again.

The whole congregation of the Israelites set out from Elim; and Israel came to the wilderness of Sin, which is between Elim and Sinai, on the fifteenth day of the second month after they had departed from the land of Egypt. The whole congregation of the Israelites complained against Moses and Aaron in the wilderness. The Israelites said to them, "If only we had died by the hand of the Lord in the land of Egypt, when we sat by the fleshpots and ate our fill of bread; for you have brought us out into this wilderness to kill this whole assembly with hunger." (Exodus 16:1-3)

Again they longed for the "good old days" back in Egypt. They longed for the days of slavery and "flesh pots." Funny, how much better things looked with the passage of time. Suddenly, Egypt had become a paradise with pots full of meat and all the bread they could eat. How selective and idealized their memories had become. Of course,

God provided for them once again, although in the wilderness it would be quail instead of fleshpots and manna instead of bread. They would not grow fat on this diet, but it would sustain them.

The Israelites' grumbling and murmuring, however, did not stop here. It continued throughout their journeys in the wilderness, and at one point God fiercely responded to their almost daily complaints. God, who is slow to anger, finally said, "Enough is enough."

> Now when the people complained in the hearing of the Lord about their misfortunes, the Lord heard it and his anger was kindled. Then the fire of the Lord burned against them, and consumed some outlying parts of the camp. But the people cried out to Moses; and Moses prayed to the Lord, and the fire abated. (Numbers 11:1-2)

Prior to this, God the divine Parent bent over backward to satisfy the legitimate needs of the Israelites. God provided for their safety (the parting of the sea), for water (turning bitter water into sweet water), and for food (providing manna and quail). Then the Israelites went too far. They crossed a line. They moved from legitimate concerns to a negative, complaining, grumbling spirit, and God's anger burned so hot it singed the fringes of the camp.

## THE PROBLEM WITH GRUMBLING

Grumbling receives poor marks in the Bible. Why the low grades? Why the bad press? A number of reasons come to mind.

*Grumbling is a form of judging.*
When we grumble, we declare that someone has either not done something he or she should have done, or that he or she did something that they should not have done. When we do that, we judge another, and Jesus warns us in the Sermon on the Mount (Matthew 7:1-5) that we will be judged in the same way we judge others. That alone is a sufficient reason to grumble less. If I know I will be held to the same standard that I hold others, it motivates me to be more understanding and less critical.

*Grumbling becomes a substitute for prayer.*

God intended us to change things through prayer, not through complaining. Jesus encouraged us to ask, seek, and knock (Matthew 7:7-8), not grumble, grouse, and gripe. When we spend much of our time complaining, we have less time for praying.

*Grumbling undermines community.*

Like termites, grumblers eat away at the foundation of community. Seldom do grumblers confront the issue or the person face-to-face. Instead, they often gripe behind the scenes. Because grumblers seldom take their concerns to those who can resolve them, issues never get resolved.

As a pastor, I witnessed many things get blown out of proportion simply because the issue was not brought to the church board or to me. Grumblers upset with something in the church would start wildfires throughout the congregation, getting others needlessly upset. Feelings would escalate, and much energy would be expended in putting out the fires. If the grumblers would have only come to us directly, many of the issues could have been resolved on the spot without upsetting so many people.

I remember the pastor who held up an egg during the children's sermon. She said, "The shell of an egg is pretty strong. Why do you think that is so? It is so the hen can sit on it without breaking. Because of its rounded shape, it is quite strong. So, how do you think a baby chick can peck its way out? A chick finds it easy to pick its way through the shell from the inside.

"The shell resists pressure from the outside, but from the inside it is easily cracked, and the little chick can get out. It took a pretty smart God to think of that, huh?"

She went on to say, "In the same way, a church (or a family) can resist outside pressure and persecution as long as they hold together in love. But when they start picking on one another, the integrity of their church (or family) is easily broken."

*Grumbling hurts the grumbler.*

A friend of mine works with salespeople. Companies call him in to light a fire under low-producing sales force. In his work he has discovered a high correlation between low producers and high negativity. He finds most low producers to be dour and cynical, and they complain constantly about the state of the company.

I think of the woman who dreamed she was being chased by a large, ugly, terrifying monster. The monster chased her everywhere, breathing down her neck, uttering ghastly sounds. In an attempt to escape, she ran into a canyon that proved to be a cul-de-sac. With her back to the canyon wall, the monster inched closer and closer and closer. When the monster was just a foot away, she cried out, "What horrible thing are you going to do to me?"

The monster stopped, looked at her, and said, "I don't know, lady, it's your dream."

To an extent our lives are like that woman's dream. Much of the time—not all the time, but much of the time—we can determine how our lives will be played out. If we adopt a grumbling spirit, we can almost assure ourselves of an uphill battle.

*Grumblers earn a bad reputation.*

Even grumblers know this. When a parishioner of mine complained to my secretary that I did not seem appreciative of her particular ministry, my secretary encouraged her to speak to me about the matter. The parishioner replied, "No, I don't want him to think I am a complainer." Few want that label for themselves.

Unfortunately, nothing is easier than fault-finding. A long time friend and mentor of mine, Alan Loy McGinnis wrote of such a person:

> I once knew a man who was married to a stunningly attractive woman, then he left her for a woman in his office whom people described as "a little frumpy." It was a reverse stereotype, for rather than leaving his wife to have an affair with some sexy, younger woman, he was doing just the opposite.
>
> I was appointed to "talk some sense into him," but I didn't get very far. The reason for his move, he explained, was simple. He couldn't handle his wife's negativism any longer. Their evenings were spent listening to her complaints. When they were in a restaurant, she was constantly critical. He never did anything right. Eventually this black cloud became too much for him.
>
> His new love, he said, might not be any good looker, but she loved him without qualification, "and when she opens her mouth, it's usually to say something cheerful," he said. "If I meet her after work for dinner, she tells me what went wrong or irritated her at

work, she doesn't hide that; but mostly we talk about good things that happened, a funny thing someone said, her appreciation for some quality in one of her colleagues."[1]

## GOOD NEWS PEOPLE

The last direction Jesus gave to his disciples was to become "good news" people. He told them, "Go into all the world and proclaim good news" (Mark 16:15). What are "good news" people? They focus on success, not failure. They look for solutions, not problems. They build bridges rather than burst bubbles. Someone once said, "Any fool can criticize, condemn, and complain—and most do!" That's a "bad news" person. They grumble, they whine, they see the glass as half-empty.

"Bad news" people are like the circus ringmaster who was approached by a man looking for work. "I'm a high-wire artist, and I'd appreciate a job," he said. Before the ringmaster could protest, the man climbed the ladder to the top of the tent, and then, without a net below him, rode a bicycle to the middle of the wire, where he remained stationary and in perfect balance.

"You guys are a dime a dozen," yelled up the ringmaster. "I'm not interested."

The man got off the bike and stood on his head on the bicycle seat.

"I've seen that a million times," yelled the ringmaster.

The man calmly pulled out a trumpet and proceeded to play Dixieland tunes while the other circus workers cheered. Then he rode the bike back to the ladder and climbed down. "Well?" he asked.

"I'll think about it," the ringmaster replied. "Let's face it; Louis Armstrong you ain't."

That ringmaster could find fault in anything. The opposite, however, is true of "good news" people. "Good news" people take you up, not down—and I'm trying to become one. I don't want to be like that cranky old Christian who died and went to heaven. Legend has it that his first comment on arrival at his celestial home was, "The halo doesn't fit!"[2] To guard against becoming that kind of person, I have to work continually on three things.

*First, I have to work on emphasizing what's right and not what's wrong.*

Best-selling author and motivational speaker Denis Waitley often speaks to high school students. One day he showed them the headline in the *Boston Globe* for November 13, 1857. The headline read, "Energy Crisis Looms." The subhead read, "World to Go Dark? Whale Blubber Scarce!" He then describes a scenario back in 1857 where the husband picks up the paper, reads the headline, and says to his wife, "Honey, we are facing the worst energy crisis in history!" The students get a good laugh out of the headline, but they also get something else. They begin to understand how easy it is to believe the sky is falling. They begin to understand society's propensity to place too much emphasis on what's wrong with our world.[3] They begin to take negative reporting with a grain of salt.

A zillion thoughts go through our minds each day, some positive and some negative. In the morning we can focus on our poor night's sleep, or our daughter's unmade bed, or the trash that was not taken out the night before . . . or we can focus on the joy of living, and the cool morning breeze, and the myriad of fresh opportunities the new day brings. The choice is ours.

I love my friend Hank Davidson. We meet every Monday for lunch. I look forward to our time together because he is the quintessential "good news" person. He continually focuses on what is right rather than what is wrong. Years ago we went on an "all sports weekend" together. We flew out to Southern California on a Thursday morning and returned on Sunday night. While in California, we attended a Dodgers baseball game, a Padres baseball game, the horse races in Del Mar, a Nebraska-UCLA football game, and a Detroit Lions-Los Angeles Rams football game. We had a great time together, and each day was an adventure for Hank—even on smoggy, overcast days. Everything was the best he had ever experienced, even when his beloved Huskers lost to my Bruins! I remember his saying, "We lost, but it was great being in the Rose Bowl, and great being together. I can't remember when I've had so much fun." When we got caught in Rose Bowl traffic after the game, and ended up going in the opposite direction from where we needed to go, he said, "This is great! I'm getting to see more of Pasadena than if we had gone the way we had planned." When we ended up staying in a rather seedy motel near the beach in San Diego, he said, "Boy, I'm glad our wives are not here. They would hate this place, but think how much money we are saving by staying in a place like this!" For Hank, every cloud has a silver lining. Years later, when I was a little squeamish about some surgery to improve my hearing, he said, "Just think how much better you will be able to hear me after it's over." And he was right.

Every crisis or heartache in life presents us with a choice. For example, my friend Lois Wade suffers from chronic back pain. Numerous trips to doctors and pain specialists have not brought her relief. She decided to bring something good out of it. She does not deny her pain. She does not put a smile on her difficulties and say everything is okay. Instead, she formed a small group for others who suffer from chronic illness or pain. She created something positive out of a great negative in her life.

*Second, I work on accepting what I cannot change.*

W.C. Fields once said, "If at first you don't succeed, try again. If the second time you still don't succeed, try once again. But if the third time you do not succeed, quit. There's no use being a fool about it." In Alcoholics Anonymous they say, "Change what you can, and accept what you can't."

A time comes when we just have to pack up and move on. The problem with grumbling is we get stuck. We never move on. We keep going over the same ground again and again. The rock group Eagles' offer wise counsel in one of their songs. They sing, "Get over it!" At times we need to do that very thing. We need to get over it. We need to let go and move on with our lives.

The Tusculani, a people of Italy, once offended the Romans. That was a dangerous thing because the power of Rome could easily wipe out a small group of people. As the Roman armies approached, the Tusculani decided upon a way to deal with them. Rather than fight, they opened the gates of their city. The men of the city unlocked all of their shops and homes. Every man, woman, and child in that city went about their daily business. When Camillus, the General of the attacking army, reached the city, he was absolutely dumbfounded. The General stood in the town square and said, "You only, of all people, have found out the true method of abating Roman fury. Your submission has proved your best defense. Upon these terms, we can no more find it in our heart to injure you than upon other terms you could have found if you had opposed us."[4]

Grumbling and griping and grousing have a way of being like those Romans. Once we decide to no longer fight, but rather to accept what we cannot change, we can get on with our lives, without suffering additional devastation and pain.

*Third, I work on practicing the art of contentment.*

A mother and son were outside when a tornado surprised them. The mother clung to a tree and tried to hold her son. But the swirling winds carried him into the sky. He was gone.

The woman began to weep and pray: "Please, O Lord, bring back my boy! He's all I have. I'd do anything not to lose him. If you'll bring him back, I'll serve you all my days."

Suddenly the boy toppled from the sky, right at her feet—a bit mussed up, but safe and sound. His mother joyfully brushed him off.

Then she stopped, looked to the sky, and said, "He had a hat, Lord."

Her contentment was short lived. So was the late Wilt Chamberlain's. Wilt Chamberlain had great numbers as an NBA star, but the number he will probably be remembered for most is 20,000. That is how many women the never-married Chamberlain claimed in his autobiography to have slept with.

What few may remember though, says columnist Clarence Page, is Chamberlain "went on to write that he would have traded all 20,000 for the one woman he wanted to stay with for keeps."[5]

In one of his early essays, Catholic writer Walter Percy captured the discontentment of our times:

> Why is a man apt to feel bad in a good environment, say suburban Short Hills, New Jersey, on an ordinary Wednesday afternoon? Why is the same man apt to feel good in a very bad environment, say an old hotel on Key Largo during a hurricane?
>
> Why is it that a man riding a good commuter train from Larchmont to New York, whose needs and drives are satisfied, who has a good home, loving wife and family, good job, who enjoys unprecedented "cultural and recreational facilities," often feels bad without knowing why?
>
> Why is the good life which men have achieved ... so bad that only news of world catastrophes, assassinations, plane crashes, mass murders, can divert one from the sadness of ordinary mornings?[6]

A partial answer to the why has to do with advertising. A multi-billion dollar industry works overtime getting us to crave what we do not have, or even need! Madison-Avenue types will lie awake tonight figuring out how they can get us to buy their product. They will be thinking of ways to inflame our passions, excite our senses for the purpose of creating enough of a desire for their product that we will feel unfulfilled without it. And talk about effective! If you slept with a roof over your head and own an automobile, you rank in the top two percent of people on this planet when it comes to material goods. Yet, how many of us want more? How many of us feel short-changed?

Is there a cure? Before C. S. Lewis began writing all his Christian works, he wrote a remarkable little book entitled *An Experiment in Criticism.* It's a book about how to read a book, and in it Lewis devoted a section to the subject of censorship. He asked, "How do we protect young people—for that matter people at large—from bad influences?" His prescription was simple: the best cure for bad literature is good literature.[7]

The same could be said about grumbling. The best cure for a bad thought is a good thought. Instead of complaining about what we do not have, we can choose to think about all the wonderful things we do have. On a trip to Brazil, I was struck by the great poverty in some areas. Yet many of those folk seemed happier than middle-class Americans. As I pondered why, I realized that they focused on what they had, not what they did not have. Like the Apostle Paul, they had learned to be content with whatever they had (Philippians 4:11).

Think of all the "natural highs" in life:[8]

Falling in love.
Laughing until your face hurts.
A hot shower.
Taking a drive on a scenic road.
Hearing your favorite song on the radio.
Lying in bed listening to the rain outside.
Hot towels out of the dryer.
A chocolate milkshake.
A bubble bath.
Giggling.
A good conversation.
The beach.
Finding a $20 bill in your coat from last winter.
Running through sprinklers.
Friends.
Accidentally overhearing someone say something
      nice about you.

Waking up and realizing you still have
    a few hours left to sleep.
Playing with a new puppy.
Spending time with old friends.
Having someone play with your hair.
Swinging on swings.
The smell of baby powder.
Watching a good movie.
Song lyrics printed inside your new CD so you can sing along.
Going to a really good concert.
Getting butterflies in your stomach every time
    you see that one person.
Winning a really competitive game.
Making chocolate chip cookies.
Holding hands with someone you care about.
Running into an old friend and realizing
    some things never change.
Riding the best roller coasters over and over.
Hugging the person you love.
Watching a sunrise.
Watching the expression on someone's face as they
    open a much-desired present.
Getting out of bed every morning and thanking God
    for another day.

Think of these things and stop grumbling!


## GROUP DISCUSSION AND SHARING

1. **Icebreaker** *(10-20 minutes)*

   • From the list of "natural highs" at the end of the chapter, which three would you place at the top of your list?

2. **Discussion** *(20-40 minutes)*

   • What is the difference between having a legitimate concern and grumbling?

   • How does it strike you that God finally said, "Enough is enough" to the Israelites? Do you think God ever does that today?

- What contributes to a grumbling or grousing mind set and spirit? Self-esteem? Upbringing? Selfishness? Control?
- What additional comments would you like to make about the chapter?

3. **Sharing** *(20-40 minutes)*

- On a scale of 1 to10, where would you place yourself when it comes to grumbling? Why there?
- How can the group be praying for you in the days ahead?

4. **Praying** *(10-15 minutes)*

Close in prayer as you normally would. If you are looking for another way of praying for one another, try praying in twosomes. Put everyone's name in a hat. Have people pick names out of the hat until everyone has a prayer partner. The partners face one another, join hands, and briefly pray for each other.

CHAPTER FIVE

# AGREE WITH ONE ANOTHER

I appeal to you, brothers, in the name of our Lord Jesus
Christ, that all of you agree with one another so that there
may be no divisions among you and that you may be
perfectly united in mind and thought.
1 Corinthians 1:10 NIV

When the Apostle Paul wrote, "I *appeal* to you ... that all of you agree with one another," what prompted him to write? What was happening in first Church Corinth?

The tone of Paul's request sounds grave. He exudes a sense of urgency and import. One definition of the word "appeal" is "an earnest request; a plea; a summons or challenge." In fact, one translation actually has Paul "pleading" rather than "appealing" to the Corinthians. Paul sounds seriously concerned about something. What has caused his distress?

In October of 1999, my wife, Trudy, and I took a group to Greece and Turkey to follow in the steps of the Apostle Paul. I had wanted to make that trip since 1972. That was the year Dr. Ralph Martin, my New Testament theology professor, showed his classes slides of Ephesus, Philippi, and Corinth. I suppressed a laugh as I watched slide after slide of the proper Dr. Martin dressed in Bermuda shorts, black knee-length socks, and loafers. What a fashion statement! What impressed me, however, were the ancient ruins of New Testament cities. I vowed that someday I would stand where Dr. Martin had stood. I would walk where Paul had walked. I also vowed never to wear Bermuda shorts with black knee-length socks and loafers!

Most people come back from Greece and Turkey most impressed with Ephesus—as well they should. The ruins in Ephesus are spectacular. The library. The amphitheater. Mary's home. The underground passage to the brothel. These sites take your breath away, but I was most impressed by the ruins in Corinth because I have been most drawn to Paul's letter to the Corinthians.

The First Church Corinth was the most successful of all of Paul's churches—at least in terms of numbers. More people embraced the good news of Jesus Christ in Corinth than in any of Paul's other churches. The success caught him by surprise. Paul came to Corinth from Athens where, according to most biblical scholars, he had failed miserably. He found few converts in that hotbed of intellectual thought. His philosophical sermon on "Mars Hill" tickled the mind, but it did not touch many hearts, and so Paul left Athens vowing to change his preaching tactics. On the road to Corinth, he decided to return to basics. No more would he attempt lofty words or wisdom to win people to Christ. Instead, he would preach the simple message of "Jesus Christ and him crucified" (1 Corinthians 2:2). He came to Corinth with knees knocking. He said that he came "in weakness and in fear and in much trembling" (1 Corinthians 2:3). He feared he might be laughed out of Corinth as he had been in Athens. After all, the cities were a mere fifty miles apart. They were similar in many ways, especially in their love of intellectual pursuits, but Paul decided to abandon philosophical arguments and words of wisdom. Instead, he would proclaim Jesus Christ as simply and clearly as he could—and the results were staggering. People in Corinth flocked to Christ.

First Church Corinth may have been Paul's biggest church, but it was also Paul's most troublesome church, and Paul does not waste much time before addressing the problem. After his customary introduction, he gets right to the point. "I appeal to you in the name of our Lord Jesus Christ that you agree with one another." I like the way Eugene Peterson puts it in *The Message*: "I have a serious concern to bring up with you . . . I'll put it as urgently as I can: You *must* get along with each other. You must learn to be considerate of one another, cultivating a life in common."[1]

People in Corinth had a bad reputation in the ancient world, and most of it was well deserved. As a lot they were promiscuous, hard-drinking, and rowdy folk. Even at a time when public morality in the Roman Empire was at a low ebb, Corinth was notorious for its questionable morals. In 400 B.C. the poet Aristophanes coined the phrase, "to live like a Corinthian" or "to Corinthianize." It became a proverbial expression for dissolute living. Scores of fertility cults had been introduced to Corinth. The cult of Aphrodite, alone, had a thousand priestess prostitutes attached to its Corinthian temple, and many of these people brought their pasts with them into the church.

And what a church it was! One man pointed to his sleeping with his stepmother as a sign of his spiritual maturity (1 Corinthians 5).

People got drunk at the Lord's Supper (1 Corinthians 11: 21). They refused to share their food at potluck suppers (1 Cor. 11:21). Members sued one another in civil courts (1 Corinthians 6:1). Some reneged on their financial pledges (1 Corinthians 16:1). In other words, they acted like stereotypical Corinthians.

Paul had spent a year and a half with them as their pastor. While there, he taught them about Christlike living. He called them to a life of holiness. Then he went to other towns to proclaim the good news. Before long, however, he received a report that in his absence things had fallen apart in Corinth, and specifically, that serious divisions had erupted in the congregation. The verse that follows his appeal to agree with one another reads, "For it has been reported to me by Chloe's people that there are quarrels among you . . . " (1 Corinthians 1:11).

## FACTIONS IN CORINTH

Each faction identified with a particular interpretation of the gospel, and with a particular Christian leader. Each faction also had its own slogan or motto. One faction boasted, "I belong to Paul"; another boasted, "I belong to Apollos"; another bragged, "I belong to Cephas"; and still another crowed, "I belong to Christ" (1 Corinthians 1:12).

The "Paul party" probably consisted of charter members of the church. They were most likely Gentile converts, and no doubt emphasized freedom from the law. They took great pride that they were in the church from the beginning. Whether they represented a "we've always done it this way" attitude, we cannot say. After all, not all charter members of churches stand in the way of change and growth. We do know, however, that they formed their group without Paul's approval and that he distanced himself from them.

The "Apollos party" probably consisted of church members who loved Apollos' strong preaching. Luke described Apollos as "an eloquent man, well versed in the scriptures" (Acts 18:24). He hailed from Alexandria, which may give us a clue about the make up of his "party" and his style of preaching. Alexandrians interpreted the scriptures allegorically. That is to say, they looked for deeper, hidden meanings in even the most simple and straightforward verses of scripture. Even though Paul had founded the church in Corinth, some members found Apollos an impressive figure and sought to lead the church in different directions under his name.

The "Cephas party" (an Aramaic name for Peter) probably consisted of Jewish converts to Christ. Though there is no record of Peter having visited Corinth, they knew him as the primary apostle, and also as one of the leaders of the predominantly Jewish church in Jerusalem. Appalled by Gentile converts in the church who paid scant attention to Jewish customs, they formed their own group of like-minded believers. The "Cephas party" would celebrate Chanukah and Passover as well as Christmas and Easter.

We can only guess who made up the "Christ party." Wouldn't everyone want to be a part of that group? Apparently not, since Paul disparages the group. In context, it must have been a group that claimed Christ as their leader in an exclusivistic way. ("We are the ones who really belong to Christ, but we're not so sure about you").[2] In all likelihood, they come out of Greek mystery cults that stressed esoteric encounters with God. Those who did not have such spiritual experiences were viewed as second-class Christians. Think of them as super-saints who looked down their noses at others.


## FACTIONS TODAY

One wishes this were a description of church *history*. One wishes this were a one-time, never-to-be-repeated scenario from the past. Unfortunately, we have much in common with First Church Corinth. Church divisions still plague us. All we need to do is substitute "I am pro-life" or "I am pro-choice" for "I am of Paul" or "I am of Apollos." Worship wars envelop many a congregation. Heated battles break out over singing out of a hymnal or singing words projected on a screen. People can be heard saying, "I am pro-synthesizer" and "I am pro-organ." Theological differences segregate people into well-protected camps: "I am an evangelical." "I am theologically liberal." "I am charismatic." These camps spend most of their time defending their position rather than listening to another point of view. Churches split over the ordination of women or the ordination of gay people. The list could go on, and you likely have similar "divisions" in your small group. I suspect some of you are pro-life, some pro-choice. Some of you prefer traditional to contemporary worship. Some of you are conservative and some liberal. How you deal with those differences will determine the success or failure of your group.

Will you ignore them, debate them, tolerate them, or go to the mat over them? Will those differences divide you or unite you?

One thinks of the minister who returned to visit a church he had once served. He ran into Bill, who had been an elder and leader in the church, but who wasn't around anymore. The pastor asked, "Bill, what happened? You used to be there every time the doors opened."

"Well, Pastor," said Bill, "a difference of opinion arose in the church. Some of us couldn't accept the final decision, and we established a church of our own."

"Is that where you worship now?" asked the pastor.

"No," answered Bill, "we found that there, too, the people were not faithful, and a small group of us began meeting in a rented hall at night."

"Has that proven satisfactory?" asked the minister.

"No, I can't say that it has," Bill responded. "The devil was active even in that fellowship, so my wife and I withdrew and began to worship on Sunday at home by ourselves."

"Then at last you have found inner peace?" asked the pastor.

"No, I'm afraid we haven't," said Bill. "Even my wife began to develop ideas I was not comfortable with, so now she worships in the northeast corner of the living room, and I am in the southwest."[3]

For many, this story hits close to home. We have not learned how to live with our differences. They have divided us. They have fractured neighborhoods, churches, and small groups. They have caused us great pain. Paul's prescription, of course, is to "agree with one another," but what did he mean by that? How are we to live out this directive? Of all the "one another" passages in the New Testament, this one baffles me. For example, if I do not see homosexuality as a sin, and you do, am I to agree with you or are you to agree with me? If I am an evolutionist and you a creationist, which one of us gives ground? If you like Mozart and I like Amy Grant, am I to abandon my musical tastes to keep the peace? To what extent are we to agree with one another? Surely, we are not to let go of well-thought-out and deeply held views. Paul certainly did not let go of his beliefs for the sake of community. He often debated with others on points of theology and practice. Did Paul not follow what he preached? What does Paul mean for us to do here? I wish we could invite Paul over for dinner to ask him to clarify his counsel. Since that is not possible, let me take a stab at what he might be saying.

## DISAGREE WITHOUT BEING DISAGREEABLE

Since Paul celebrates the diversity of the Body of Christ later in his letter to the Corinthians, his counsel to "agree with one another" could not mean uniformity of thought. Paul accepted the fact that God gives people different gifts and passions, that God "wires" people differently. Furthermore, Paul could be as argumentative as they come. Invite Paul to dinner and you could count on lively dinner conversation. He did not mince words. Paul was an "in-your-face" kind of guy. He did not tiptoe around issues or people. If he thought you were off base, he would let you know. So what did he mean by "agreeing with one another?" I think the answer can be found in his "love" chapter:

> Love is patient; love is kind; love is not envious or boastful or arrogant or rude. It does not insist on its own way; it is not irritable or resentful; it does not rejoice in wrongdoing, but rejoices in the truth. It bears all things, believes all things, hopes all things, endures all things. (1 Corinthians 13:4-7)

Note what he says here. He says love rejoices in the truth, not in wrongdoing. In other words, love will disagree at times—*but* without being disagreeable. Love disagrees kindly and patiently, not rudely or arrogantly.

Jerry Sutcliffe modeled this so beautifully. Jerry opposed the building expansion in our congregation. Actually, he opposed the financing of the plan. He thought the mortgage was much too high. He stood before the congregation and told us so. He did so with passion and integrity. He believed we were biting off more than we could chew, and he wanted to postpone building until we had raised more money. The congregation disagreed with him and voted to proceed with the expansion. The next day he resigned from the Board of Trustees because he, in good conscience, could not sign loan documents for the project. But he continued to teach his adult Sunday School class. He continued to worship regularly. He continued to offer us pro bono legal counsel. He definitely disagreed with us, but he was never disagreeable.

Neither was Betty Kimbrel. Betty came into my office disappointed with a decision we had made. She objected to the firing of one of our custodians. The custodian had a big heart, but he required much too much supervision. I told her our reason for the termination, and she said, "I disagree with your rationale. As a church we could have done more for Brad. Surely, we could have found someone who could have given him the guidance he required." With that she said, "I won't take up any more of your time. Thank you for allowing me to speak my piece." She shook my hand and walked out of the office. She disagreed without being disagreeable, and she never brought up the matter again.

Love does not rejoice in wrongdoing. Love rejoices in the truth, and it does so without being rude or arrogant.


## REACH OUT TO YOUR ENEMIES

Love also reaches out to enemies. I'm sure Paul had this thought in mind as well when he pleaded with the Corinthians to "agree with one another." As followers of Christ, what do we agree to do? We agree to embrace those who disagree with us. Of course, embracing our enemies presents us with a dilemma. By that I mean, who wants to do it? Let me remind you of Jesus' words:

> But I say to you that listen, Love your enemies, do good
> to those who hate you, bless those who curse you, pray
> for those who abuse you. (Luke 6:27-28)

Be honest. How many of us get excited about loving our enemies? How many of us look forward to being nice to those who have hurt us? How many of us enjoy blessing rather than cursing our foes? How many of us take pleasure in embracing our opponents? My guess is, not many of us, and I would venture to say that "loving one's enemies" is the least appealing commandment in the Bible. Can you think of another commandment of Jesus' that is less attractive? I can't.

In the Greek language there are four words for love. There is *storge,* which is parental affection for a child. There is *eros,* which refers to romantic love. There is *phileo,* from which we get the word "Philadelphia." It refers to brotherly or sisterly love, the kind of love we share with friends. Finally there is *agape* love, which is the word Jesus uses here. Now, this is crucial to understand. The first three Greek words for love—*storge, phileo, eros*—are emotionally charged words. They are feeling words. But not so with *agape. Agape* love is not a feeling. Rather it is a state of the mind or an act of the will. So, thankfully, Jesus does not say that we have to *feel* loving toward our enemies, we just need to *act* loving toward them. Jesus does not ask us to love our enemies as we love those nearest and dearest to us. We are just to act with love toward them, and he goes on to mention three ways we are to do this.

*Number one, we are to do good to them.*

If our enemy thirsts, we are to offer him something to drink. If our enemy hungers, we are to offer her something to eat. If we are having trouble with a co-worker or neighbor, we are to look for ways to meet their legitimate needs. Think of an enemy. Got that person in mind? Now think of something good you could do for him or her. Does it make you want to gag? But that's what Jesus asks us to do.

*Number two, we are not only supposed to do good things to them, we are also to speak well of them: Bless those who curse you.*

I think of the two men who ran a close race for public office. After the election a reporter told the loser of all the demeaning things the winner had said about him and asked if he would care to comment. He thought for a minute, remembered this injunction of Jesus, and said, "Well, for a man who sweats like a pig, he doesn't smell too bad."

That's not what Jesus had in mind. My mother gave me a piece of advice more times than I can count. She would say, "If you can't say anything nice, do not say anything at all." That's a good thought, but Jesus counsel goes beyond my mother's counsel. Jesus doesn't tell me to bite my tongue. That does not go far enough. He tells me to think of good things about my enemies and say them.

*Number three, we are to pray for those who abuse us.*

Now this sounds a lot better. We can do this. We can pray that God's judgment will fall upon them. We can pray for some misfortune to come upon them. We can pray that others treat them as badly as they have treated us. Right? Wrong. What Jesus wants us to pray is more like this: "O God, I pray that you will enormously bless this person. I pray that she might be led to worship you. I pray for her spiritual growth. I pray that this person will come to love you with all their heart, soul, strength, and mind." In other words, whoever is an enemy, add him or her to your prayer list. Pray for that person who drives you up a wall.

As I write this, I smile at God's sense of timing—or humor! Someone has been a pain in my petunia for the past three months. Whenever I think of this person, my blood boils. Actually, I fluctuate between fury and pity. At times I pity the person because of his insecurity. Other times, I feel like screaming at him. So what happens? We end up in the same small group! God puts the two of us together on the same presbytery committee! For the next two years I get to embrace an enemy. I get to do good things with him. I get to say good things about him. I get to pray for him. Let me be honest. I do not relish the idea of doing this. Like the people in First Church Corinth, I would much rather divorce myself from this person. I would much rather go my way and he go his way, but the Apostle Paul calls the two of us to "agree with one another." What does that mean for us? It means we agree to act loving toward each other. We will probably never become bosom buddies. We will no doubt always harbor some hurt and bitter feelings toward one another, but God has placed us in community together. We do not want the quarrels and divisions between us to define the church or us. So, we have agreed to act with love toward one another. I think that would put a smile on Paul's face.

## PRIZE UNITY AS MUCH AS PURITY

Thirdly, I think Paul is telling us here to prize unity as much as purity. Of course, that's as big a challenge as loving one's enemies because many value purity.

I think of the man who was shipwrecked and found himself washed up on an island. He searched around and found he was the sole inhabitant. After thinking about the situation, he got busy and began making do for himself.

One day, a number of years later, as he was scanning the horizon, he saw a big yacht. Awhile later a dinghy carried two people to his island. He was so excited to see people that he ran down to the shore and began greeting them before they even landed. He asked them if they would like to see the accommodations he had made for himself. "Sure," they replied, "show us."

He led them into the interior of the island where there was a cluster of buildings. "That one," he pointed, "is my house."

"What's that one," they asked as they pointed to a large structure.

"That's my barn. I've domesticated some of the goats on the island, and I keep some of the tools I've made there."

"What's that building?" they asked, as they pointed to another building.

"Oh, that's my church. I get spiritual sustenance when I go there to worship."

"What's that other building?" they asked, as they pointed to another structure.

"Oh," he said, "that's where I used to go to church."

Now, that guy values spiritual purity! When he disagrees with *himself,* he changes churches! But what about unity? How would he fair in a theologically or culturally diverse congregation? Would his desire for purity outweigh his desire for unity?

I am in a national covenant group with church growth pastors from across the United States. Joe Rightmyer is one of the guys in my small group. Joe serves as President of Presbyterians for Renewal, a conservative branch of our denomination. He travels across the country addressing some of the "hot topics" facing our church. He often finds himself pitted against others who have a different view of the spiritual direction of our denomination. In all the years I have known him, however, he has never encouraged the conservatives to leave the denomination, even though he disagrees strongly with many of the stances taken by our General Assembly. He encourages his constituents to value unity as much as purity.

Now, Joe and I differ theologically. Joe is a little more biblically conservative than I, but I appreciate his spirit, and I agree with his message: prize unity as much as purity. Focus on what unites us, rather than what divides us. Learn how to live together amidst our differences. For Joe, as was the case with the Apostle Paul, birds of different feathers can flock together.

## BE READY TO FORGIVE AND BE FORGIVEN

Finally, when Paul asks us to "agree with one another," I think he's asking us to be ready to forgive and be forgiven. When people hurt us, our natural tendency is to strike back, retaliate, reciprocate. That, of course, wreaks havoc with community. It fosters "disagreeability" rather than "agreeability."

For a number of years, Bob Knight was an institution at Indiana University. He coached Indiana to three NCAA basketball championships and 763 victories. His twenty-nine-year career ended at Indiana when he was fired on September 15, 2000. The university dismissed its longtime coach after a nineteen-year-old student claimed that Knight had grabbed his arm and lectured him about manners. This action violated the "no tolerance" policy imposed on Knight by the university four months earlier. This was not an isolated incident. In 1979 Knight was convicted of hitting a Puerto Rican policeman during a team practice session at the Pan American Games. During a game versus Purdue in 1985, he tossed a chair across the court nearly hitting people sitting in the wheelchair section. In 1986 he kicked a megaphone and swore at cheerleaders during a game against Illinois. In 1997 Knight allegedly choked a former player during practice. In 1998 Knight swore at an athletic department secretary and advanced toward her in anger before athletic director Clarence Doninger interceded. As part of the "zero tolerance" policy, the university encouraged Knight to take an anger management course, but he refused. He told the university he did not have a problem with anger. After the firing, he threatened to sue the university for defamation of character.

If he had asked for forgiveness, he would have been able to stay. Knight, however, was not ready to be forgiven. In his eyes, he had done nothing wrong. If he had been ready to forgive, history would have judged him in a more positive light. Instead, Knight came off as an angry, stubborn, unforgiving human being, and his relationship with Indiana University was severed irreparably.

It's impossible to maintain community without forgiveness. We maintain community by offering it and receiving it.

So, if the Apostle Paul were at our dinner party, that's what I think he would have said when we asked him about "agreeing with one another." I think he would have said, it means disagreeing without being disagreeable, reaching out to our enemies, prizing unity as much as purity, and being ready to forgive and be forgiven. If you see Paul before I do, ask him if we captured the gist of what he was saying. See if he agrees with this take on his appeal.

## GROUP DISCUSSION AND SHARING

1. **Icebreaker** *(20-30 minutes)*
   - Share something you happily agreed to do.
   - Share something you reluctantly agreed to do.

2. **Discussion** *(20-40 minutes)*
   - What do you think of the church in Corinth? In what ways is it similar to your church or fellowship? Dissimilar?
   - In your opinion, do those outside the church see church people as agreeable and unified or disagreeable and factious? Explain.
   - How close do you think this chapter comes to capturing the gist of what Paul meant to "agree with one another?" Where is it on the mark? Where does it miss?
   - How can your group practice this "one another" command? What will it entail for your small group to "agree with one another?"

3. **Sharing** *(15-35 minutes)*
   - Rank the following from 1 to 4, with one being the most difficult for you to do:

     ____ Disagree without being disagreeable

     ____ Reach out to my enemies

     ____ Prize unity as much as purity

     ____ Be ready to forgive and being forgiven
   - How can the group be praying for you?

4. **Praying** *(5-15 minutes)*
   Close in prayer as you normally do, or pray for the person on your left. Give group members a short time to write their prayer for the person. After a couple of moments, have each member read their prayer for their assigned person. Do this with eyes open, focusing attention on the person being prayed for. Remember that God hears prayers, even when we do not close our eyes! The group leader ends the time by simply saying, "Amen."

CHAPTER SIX

# LOOK OUT FOR ONE ANOTHER

Let each of you look not to your own interests,
but to the interests of others.
Philippians 2:4

In the 2000 presidential campaign, Senator John McCain made a strong bid for the oval office. After the scandals of the Clinton presidency, the Senator's strength of character attracted many. Even opponents respected the depth and courage of his values. During the election, his biography captured America's attention, especially the story of how he could have been released by Hanoi as a prisoner of war but refused to go unless his comrades were freed as well. What kind of person would do that? What kind of person would sacrifice his own well being for that of his friends? What kind of person puts the needs of others on equal footing with his or her own?

Thankfully, McCain is not alone when it comes to looking out for the interests of others. Take Larry Deans. Larry, an eighty-year-old retiree, chaired the Personnel Committee of our church. Shortly after my coming to the church, he heard the story of how I had completed all the course work for a doctor of ministry degree but had not written the dissertation. Instead of the dissertation, I had written *One Anothering, Volume 1.* Small groups had exploded in our congregation, and providing a starter series for small groups seemed more pressing than the completion of academic work. I rationalized the delay by saying, "When I get the book done, I will get back to the dissertation." That did not happen. Instead, I got further sidetracked. I lost an associate, and thus my pastoral workload increased while we searched for his replacement. Then came building projects and campaigns. I hardly had enough time for my family, let alone a dissertation. Ultimately, I missed the deadline. If I wanted to complete my degree, I needed to update my course work or the seminary had to grant me an extension.

Larry asked, "If the seminary granted you an extension without additional course work, would you write the dissertation?" I said, "Of course. It would be good to have it done. I was so close."

Months later Larry called and asked if he could drop by my office. He told me it wouldn't take long. He came bearing a file folder. He handed it to me and said, "With the help of your wife, I contacted the seminary. I told them of your situation and asked if they would grant an extension. After researching your file, they sent it along to the appropriate approval committee. The committee knew of your work in small groups and said that because you have remained current in church renewal issues, they would give you a two-year window to complete the dissertation. All you need to do is call this woman, at this number, and she will tell you what to do next."

I was flabbergasted. I could not believe what Larry had done for me, and every time I look at the diploma I now have, I think of him and the smile he had on his face the day he handed me that file folder. If it had not been for him, I doubt that I would have earned the degree.

I also think of a time when my mother was looking out for me, even though I did not know it or appreciate it when it happened. I was sixteen years old and had been invited by my best friend, Karl LaCom, to travel to San Diego, attend a car show, spend the night, and come back the next day. What a trip it would be! This was before the days of Steve Martin and Dan Ackroyd, but we just knew we would be "two wild and crazy guys." My mother must have intuitively known our hopes for our overnight excursion because she nixed the idea. She felt I was too young to travel one hundred miles south without a chaperone. I begged and pleaded, but she held her ground. At the time, I thought I had the strictest mother in all of Glendale, California. Now, after having children of my own, I know she had only my best interests at heart. Two sixteen-year-old boys, a hundred miles from home, on their own, without adult supervision was a recipe for disaster. She was simply looking out for me.

Who looks out for you? Who do you look out for?

## LOVING OUR NEIGHBOR

Jesus put it this way: "You shall love your neighbor as yourself" (Matthew 22:39). He uttered these words in response to one of life's big questions: Which demands upon our time are most imperative? Wouldn't you like to know that? Wouldn't you like to know how to prioritize your life? Wouldn't you like to move from "motion without meaning" to "focus with a purpose"?

This "demands" question came immediately after two other important questions. In rapid succession three tough questions were posed to Jesus. The first question (Matthew 22:17) came from some Pharisees: "Is it lawful to pay taxes to the emperor or not?" Good question, and oh, how I wish he had said, "No!" I dread April 15th. How about you? Trudy and I have often miscalculated our quarterly IRS payments, requiring us to come up with balloon payments on the 15th. Each balloon payment affected our budget for the entire year. In fact, we are still recovering from a large shortage a few years back! We might not like the answer, but Jesus tells us to be good citizens by paying our taxes. "Give to the emperor the things that are the emperor's" (Matthew 22:21).

The second question came from the Sadducees. They had life after death on their minds. They described a scenario where a woman is widowed seven times, and they inquired of Jesus, "In the resurrection, then, whose wife of the seven will she be? For all of them had married her?" (Matthew 22:28). We still wonder about life after death. Is there such a thing? If so, what will our bodies be like? Will we be able to recognize one another? Are there really a heaven and a hell? Will we have to play the harp or do we get our choice of instruments? Will there be golf? Will we still have to diet? Will there be hot fudge sundaes and deep dish pizza? Inquiring minds want to know.

The last question came from a lawyer. Some of my best friends are attorneys, and I do not want to disparage that fine vocation, but to be honest, I did enjoy what Malcolm Ford said about his father, Harrison Ford. Malcolm was a preschooler at the time, and in explaining what his father did for a living he said, "My daddy is a movie actor, and sometimes he plays the good guy, and sometimes he plays the lawyer." The lawyer who approached Jesus was one of "those" lawyers. He wasn't seeking the truth. He wasn't asking his question in order to learn and grow in his faith. This lawyer already knew the answer. He just wanted to "test" Jesus, to trip him up, and he asked him, "Teacher, what commandment of the law is the greatest?" (Matthew 22:36).

With scarcely a breath in between, Jesus answered the man by quoting the Shema (Deuteronomy 6:5), which faithful Jews recited twice daily, and he matched it with the commandment in Leviticus 19:18: "You shall love your neighbor as yourself." Jesus said all the prophets and all the law can be boiled down to these two commandments: Love God with every fiber of your being—mind, heart, soul, strength—and love your neighbor as yourself.

I like what my friend Dale Bruner says about Jesus' answer to the greatest commandment.

> It must be stressed for the sake of a clear appreciation of Jesus' point that Jesus had *not* been asked for the *two* main commandments in the law; he had only been asked the single main commandment. When, therefore, Jesus gratuitously gives a *second* answer to a question asking for a single answer, he is saying in so many words that the question for *one* main principle is too narrow. Jesus' double answer can heal a division—the division between the evangelical and the social wings of the church. In whichever wing we feel most comfortable, we repeatedly hear the absolutizing of one of the two commanded loves. And the not always explicit but usually implicit suggestion is the lesser importance of the other love . . . the spiritual and the social cannot be separated . . . Just as it is not true that love of God is the *only* important commandment (against the spiritualizers), so it is also not true that only love of neighbor *is* love of God (against the secularizers). Only together in a nurturing mutuality is either love kept pure.[1]

So, what demands on our time are most imperative? How are we to prioritize our lives? Jesus said by loving God and cherishing others as ourselves. What does it mean to love our neighbor as our self? What does it mean to look out not only for our own interests, but also for the interests of others?

## DANGER #1: LOVING TOO MUCH

Loving our neighbor does not mean loving them *more* than we love ourselves. Jesus did not say, "Love your neighbor *more* than yourself." He said, "Love your neighbor *as* yourself." Jesus' command both clarifies and softens the words of Paul. Paul counseled the Philippians, "Let each of you look not to your own interests, but to the interests of others" (Philippians 2:4). Taking these words literally, Paul appears to be saying, "Always put the interests of others before your own." "Don't focus on yourself. Focus on others." "Be *other* directed." If he meant that, he was wrong. Always putting others before ourselves eventually leads to exhaustion.

I carry this truth in my head, but not in my heart, and it was the primary reason for my leaving pastoral ministry. I had difficulty saying "No" to people, and when I did say it, I felt guilty. Taking time for myself seemed selfish. The needs of the people were great: deaths, divorces, illnesses, worries, and disappointments. How could I not respond to the pain? How could I turn my back on legitimate needs to spend time with my family or read a novel or play a round of golf? And words like, "Let each of you look not to your own interests, but to the interests of others," bore into my soul. Robert Keck talks about our LQ (Love Quotient).[2] He says our society is preoccupied with IQ (Intelligence Quotient), and our world needs to stress the importance of LQ. He thanks God that he had a mother who had both: a high IQ and a high LQ. But I never felt my LQ was very high when I resented the calls in the middle of the night and the crises that demanded immediate attention. Based on Jesus' words, I know I was not being selfish by looking out for my own interests; I knew that taking time for myself was important. I just could not get that thought to move those eighteen inches from my head into my heart.

I marvel at how Jesus had the ability to walk away from the crowds. He fed thousands. He healed hundreds, but he did not respond to every need. He was never too busy to be interrupted, but he was never so available that he always dropped everything. He took time for himself. He spent time alone with God. He savored time with his friends. He attended dinner parties.

It's okay to take care of ourselves. Note what Morton Kelsey, an Episcopal priest and counselor, does to refresh his spirit.

> I also find that once a year I need a period of at least thirty-six hours of total quiet and reflection. After a very busy time I may need longer, sometimes a week, or even a month. I have found that after many months of intensive work it may take several weeks before I can unwind and the depth of me begins to be revealed. Jung said that after three months of continuously listening to people in their agony and confusion he needed a month away to unpoison himself. It can also be helpful for others whom we are counseling or guiding to learn to get along without us, and good for our

humility to realize that they can.  This does not mean that we leave our family and other personal responsibilities behind.  Rather we are given a fresh look at these aspects of life.

During this period we are sometimes given entirely new perspectives on who we are and how God wants us to serve. We may need to draw up a new list of priorities.[3]

We need to take care of ourselves because caring for others is both fulfilling *and* draining. To love others, we need to love ourselves. We need to make sure we are filling our bucket so that others can drink out of it. When our bucket dries up, we have nothing left to give anyone.

I think of the man who was building a home in Vermont in a place where it is very difficult to get water. He asked an old Vermonter to come over and divine the source of water on his property with a stick, so he could dig a well. Sure enough, this old-timer found the appropriate spot. "Just dig fourteen feet straight down, and you will find an underground river. When you hit water, pump it out every day."

The man followed the instructions and found the underground river. He pumped it out the first day and more water came in. In the next few days the water rose four feet, then six feet, then eight feet. At eight feet the well seemed stationary, so he left it. Returning some months later when the house was finished, he immediately turned on the water. The first day there seemed to be plenty, but by the next day there was none at all. The well was dry.

He went to see the old Vermonter to tell him the disappointing story. The old man asked, "Did you pump it out every day?"

"No," said the man.

The Vermonter shook his head and said, "You fool! An underground river is made up of thousands of little underground capillaries. As you pump water you enlarge those capillaries, and more water comes. Once you stop, the water backs up, the capillaries close, and the river is formed somewhere else."[4]

Once we stop taking care of ourselves, our river of compassion runs dry. If we are going to look out for the interests of others, we cannot ignore our own interests. We need to love others *as* we love ourselves.

## DANGER #2: LOVING TOO LITTLE

The flip side of loving ourselves is to make sure we do not concentrate *too much* on ourselves. This results in loving our neighbor less than we love ourselves, and this dangerous behavior motivated Paul, in part, to pen his words to the Philippians.

When we are concerned first and foremost with our own interest, we are bound to collide with others. That's what had happened in Philippi. Paul wrote this letter after Epaphroditus had informed him of a tendency toward a party spirit and a personal antagonism between two women that was threatening the peace in the church. He told the church to look out for one another instead of being so consumed with their own selfish concerns.

The situation in Philippi must have come as quite a shock to Paul because, of all of his churches, this was his favorite. One cannot miss the affection in his voice when he writes them. He began his letter by saying, "I thank my God every time I remember you . . . It is right for me to think this way about all of you, because you hold me in your heart" (Philippians 1:3,7). Now comes the news that disunity and disputes have crept into the fellowship. The church that had cared so much for him, and one another, had suddenly taken a wrong turn.

Jill Briscoe shared a poem in one of her sermons. Listen to it:

In the dim and distant past
When life's tempo wasn't fast,
Grandma used to rock and knit,
Crochet, tat, and baby-sit.

When the kids were in a jam,
They could always count on Gram.
In an age of gracious living,
Grandma was the gal for giving.

Grandma now is at the gym
Exercising to keep slim.
She's off touring with a bunch,
Taking clients out to lunch.
Driving north to ski or curl,
All her days are in a whirl.
Nothing seems to stop or block her,
Now that Grandma's off her rocker.[5]

Paul must have felt the Philippian church had gone off its rocker. The church who had done so much for him, the church who had cared so deeply for him, the church who had looked out for his interests, was becoming infected by a self-centeredness that was unbecoming and contrary to the example of Christ. Like Grandma, they had begun to love less.

That is easy to do and tough to fix. I am told that when young Russian children go to school, there is map of the world running across the top of the classroom blackboard, and at the very center of that map is Russia. From personal experience, when I went to school the map at the top of my classroom blackboard had the United States at its center. From early on, we place ourselves at the center of the world. Galileo was branded a heretic because he had the audacity to say that the universe did not revolve around the earth. Not long ago, a man from El Paso, Texas, boasted that his city was centrally located. "We are 600 miles east of Los Angeles, 600 miles south of Denver, and 600 miles west of San Antonio." Few of us would see El Paso as the center of the United States, but he did!

In this connection one thinks of Helmut Theilecke's understanding of Genesis 3. Adam and Eve were meant to live *from* the middle. They chose instead to live *in* the middle. That's us. We were intended to live out from the divine center. Instead, we have become the center. Remember that old saying, "What's good for General Motors is good for America"? We may not say it, but we often think it: "What's good for me is good for the world."

Freeman Patterson, an outstanding Canadian photographer, explained his method of taking pictures. His process sheds light on this discussion:

> Letting go of self is an essential precondition to real seeing. When you let go of yourself, you abandon any preconceptions about the subject matter which might cramp you into photographing in a certain, predetermined way. As long as you are worried about whether or not you will be able to make good pictures, or concerned about enjoying yourself, you are unlikely either to take the best photographs you can or experience the joy of photography to the fullest. When you let go new conceptions arise from your direct experience of the subject matter, and new ideas and feelings will guide as you make pictures.

Preoccupation with self is the greatest barrier to seeing, and the hardest one to break.[6]

Preoccupation with self is also a great barrier to community, and it's tough to break. Most of us are not too far removed from the two women who left worship on a Sunday morning. One woman said to other, "This morning's sermon about 'Only Thinking of Oneself' was really moving." The other replied, "It had quite an effect on me, too! It's the first time I didn't pray that I'd find a good man to marry! Instead, I prayed that my parents would get a good son-in-law!"

I'm a lot like that woman. I am deeply self-centered, and though I may hide the fact behind good deeds or the creative use of words, I desperately desire my own way. As one writer put it,

> Each person is like an actor who wants to run the whole show; is forever trying to manage the lights, the ballet, the scenery and the rest of the players in his own way. If his arrangements would only stay put, if only people would do as he wishes, the show would be great. Everybody, including himself, would be pleased. Life would be wonderful.[7]

What's the cure to rampant self-centeredness? It's looking out for the interests of others. It's loving neighbors as we love ourselves. Psychologist Alfred Adler once put an ad in the paper for his "Fourteen Day Cure Plan." He claimed that he could cure anyone of any emotional or mental disorder in just fourteen days. One day an extremely lonely man came in for advice. Adler told the man that if he would do as instructed, he would be cured of his loneliness in a mere fourteen days.

"What do you want me to do?" he asked.

Adler replied, "If you will do something for someone else every day for fourteen days, your loneliness will be gone."

The man objected, "Why should I do anything for someone else?"

To which the psychologist replied, tongue-in-cheek, "Well, in your case, it may take twenty-one days."[8]

Curing my self-centeredness will take more than twenty-one days! How about you?

## LOOKING OUT FOR ONE ANOTHER

Guarding against the two extremes—too much love and not enough love—Paul calls us to look out for the interests of others. How do we do that in a small group? How do we do that with those with whom we have decided to build significant community? Let me suggest some ways.

*One, we value each member's input.*

We realize that we do not have the last word or the most important word on every subject. We ask each member what he or she wants out of the group. In their book *Communicating in Small Groups,* Steven Beebe and John Masterson list twenty group roles that contribute to the health of a small group.[9] Two have to do with looking out for the interests of others. One role is that of "opinion seeker" (asks for clarification of the values and opinions expressed by other group members) and the other role is that of "encourager" (offers praise, understanding, and acceptance of others' ideas and suggestions). Try practicing one or both of these roles on a regular basis. We can hardly look out for one another's interests if we do not know what their interests are.

*Two, we make time for one another.*

Years ago a couple of psychologists speculated about the possible differences between the unhelpful priest and Levite, and the helpful Samaritan in the Parable of the Good Samaritan. They wondered why the first two didn't stop while the third one did. Their conclusion? The Samaritan was probably in less of a hurry.

Here's what they did. They created a situation similar to the scene described in the parable, and they placed some Princeton seminary students in the middle of it. Each seminary student was asked to deliver a brief talk on the story of the Good Samaritan at a recording studio across campus. While in transit they would meet a victim slumped in an alley, head down, eyes closed, coughing and groaning. Half the students were told they had plenty of time to make their appointment. The other half were told they had to get there right away because the recording would take place in five minutes.

Of the students who were told they had plenty of time to make their appointment, most of them stopped to help the man in distress. Of those who were told they had to get there in five minutes, only ten percent of them stopped. They concluded that hurried people are likely to pass by someone in distress, even if they are hurrying to speak on the parable of the Good Samaritan! The difference in helping was not due to callousness. The difference was time pressure. To make sure we do not pass by the others in our group, we need to make time for them. We cannot look out for their interests unless we set aside the necessary time.

*Three, we call people between meetings to see how they are doing.*

When someone has an important interview or doctor's appointment or matter that needs to be handled before the next group meeting, we call that person to see how things went. We want to make sure they are okay. We want to know how we can be of further assistance. We do not want to discover at the next meeting that things did not go well. We want to be there for them if they need us.

*Four, we raise a red flag when we see danger.*

If a group member is heading down the wrong road, we warn them. In Proverbs we read, "Well meant are the wounds of a friend, but profuse are the kisses of an enemy." At times, we may need to criticize a course of action. Think of it as "care-frontation." Many a time I have been spared from disaster because someone in the group had the courage to say to me, "I would not go down that road if I were you." They did not do it to hurt me. They did it because they had my best interest at heart.

I like the distinction Randy Frazee makes between tolerance and codependence in his book *The Connecting Church.* We all want to be tolerant. We do not want to push our views and opinions upon anyone else, and we do not want others to do the same to us, but Frazee points out that too much tolerance harms rather than helps. He says the difference between tolerance and codependence is determined by the nature of the behavior of the other person. After defining a codependent person as one who "enables a person to continue in his or her destructive behavior, such as alcohol or substance abuse," he writes,

> If the behavior is seen as moral and nondestructive to herself and others then the confronting person is considered tolerant; if the behavior is immoral and destructive to herself and others, then the confronting person is considered codependent.[10]

In other words, we can afford to be tolerant if the behavior is nondestructive. If we do not say anything, no one will be hurt. We cannot afford to be tolerant, however, if someone is in danger. When we allow destructive behavior to pass by without saying anything about it. we move from being tolerant people to codependent people.

*Five, we go the extra mile for people in our group.*

My wife's small group is something else. They call themselves "The Samarai Sisters." I won't get into how they got their name. What's important is how they constantly go the extra mile for one another. When Trudy had a questionable mammogram, Sandy Collins went with her for her next mammogram. Trudy, in her concern over the results of the first mammogram, did not listen closely to the time for her next x-ray. As a result, she got to the radiologist two hours early. Trudy told Sandy, "Go back home. I got the time wrong. I know you have better things to do." Sandy said, "No, I have no better place to be than here with you," and she stayed with Trudy the entire time.

*Six, we are on the lookout for what others need.*

After being with one another for a while, we get to know each other's interests, needs, and desires. Before long, we have those things in the back of our minds as we go about our daily routines. When we read the paper, watch TV, or meet someone, we do so with different eyes and ears. We do so, not only looking out for our interests, but their interests as well. In time, we begin saying things to one another such as, "I know a great counselor who might be able to help with your marriage," or "I found a great handyman the other day. Do you still need someone to help you with your deck?" or "My company has an opening for a software engineer. Are you interested?" or "I saw an ad in the paper for a side-by-side refrigerator. Do your kids still need one?" or "I heard on the news last night that interest rates have gone down. Do you still want to refinance your house?" In other words, we carry their needs and interests with us during the week, and when we see something that might interest them, we bring it to their attention.

I'm sure there are other practical ways you can look out for one another in your group, but these six suggestions give you a place to start.

## GROUP DISCUSSION AND SHARING

1.  **Icebreaker** *(20-30 minutes)*
    - Share a high point and a low point from your past week.
    - Who or what was at the center of your life when you were in elementary school? When you were in high school? College?

2.  **Discussion** *(30-40 minutes)*
    - What jumped out at you in the "Danger #1: Loving Too Much" section? In the "Danger #2: Loving Too Little" section? In the "Loving Your Neighbor" section?
    - What do you think of Adler's "Fourteen Day Cure Plan"? Will it cure self-centeredness? If so, why? If not, why not?
    - How does one strike a balance between loving too much and not loving enough?
    - What, if anything, would you add to the list under "Looking Out for One Another?" Which would you like your group to do more of?

3.  **Sharing** *(15-30 minutes)*
    Loving God and cherishing others are to be the two most important priorities in our lives.
    - What letter grade would you give yourself for loving God? For loving others?
    - How can group members be "looking out for you" in the days ahead?

4.  **Prayer** *(5-10 minutes)*
    Close in prayer as you normally do, or simply pray for the person on your left.

CHAPTER SEVEN

# SPEAK TO ONE ANOTHER WITH PSALMS, HYMNS, AND SPIRITUAL SONGS

Speak to one another with psalms, hymns and spiritual songs.
Sing and make music in your heart to the Lord,
always giving thanks to God the Father for everything,
in the name of our Lord Jesus Christ.
Ephesians 5:19-20 NIV

I did not want to do it. I did not even think I could do it. But I did not want to appear wimpy, so I answered, "No, problem!" when asked to take a cab from La Guardia Airport to my accommodations in downtown Manhattan. Granted, I grew up in a big city, Los Angeles, but take a cab? Never. Cabs were few and far between in La La Land. Everyone had his or her own vehicle. As a result, I could count on one hand the number of times I had taken a cab, and most of those times I was with my father who had grown up in nearby New Jersey. While preparing for the trip, all sorts of "cab" questions popped into my mind. Where do I pick up the cab? What if the driver senses fear in my eyes? What if he takes me to the hotel via Albany? What if the driver does not speak English? What if I do not have enough cash to pay him?

I was traveling to New York to lead a small group seminar at Marble Collegiate Church, where Norman Vincent Peale, the father of The Power of Positive Thinking, had once served. Not being the most positive person in the world (as you might have guessed from my cab story), I often read "positive thinking" material. I hope by reading people such as Norman Vincent Peale and Robert Schuller and Zig Zieglar, I might become a more optimistic person. It has not happened yet, but I have only been working on it for twenty-five years.

As usual, I did not have to worry. I easily found a cab. The trip into the city was quick and uneventful, the fare was reasonable, and to my delight the cabbie spoke English. I had only one regret. I did not experience one of those colorful, New York cab drivers that Norman Vincent Peale had written about in one of his books.[1]

One doesn't think of New York cabbies as being particularly pious, but scarcely had this man picked up Peale (the cabbie did not know his identity), when he began talking about his church and how much it meant to him and how he loved to sing in the choir on Sunday mornings. To Peale's astonishment, the cab driver broke into a familiar hymn as they rolled down Fifth Avenue. Then he began to talk again. "I haven't always been a taxi driver," he said. "I had a good business once, but it went down in the Depression. My minister got me into the taxi business. 'Bill,' he said, 'running a taxi is the same as anything else. Give good service, be friendly, treat people right, and trust in God, and you'll get along and have a good time doing it.' " The driver went on, "My minister told me that every morning when I went over to the garage to get my cab, before I started I was to bow my head over the wheel and pray. That may sound pious, but I want to tell you that I've made a good living. What's more, I've had a wonderful time, and I'm happy, happier than I've ever been before."

None of my cabbies ever broke out into song. In fact, they only spoke to me twice: once, to ask for my destination, and the other time to inform me of the amount of the fare. What a disappointment!


## BE FILLED WITH THE SPIRIT

I mention all this because the Apostle Paul encourages us to act like Peale's cab driver: to break into song when we get together. Paul's encouragement comes on the heels of his instructing us to be "filled with the Spirit." Consider his words:

> Be careful how you live, not as unwise people but as wise, making the most of the time, because the days are evil. So do not be foolish but understand what the will of the Lord is. Do not get drunk with wine, for that is debauchery; but be filled with the Spirit, as you sing psalms and hymns and spiritual songs among yourselves, singing and making melody to the Lord in your hearts, giving thanks to God the father at all times and for everything in the name of our Lord Jesus Christ. (Ephesians 5:15-20)

Have you noticed how intoxicated people often break into song when they drink together? Why is that? A number of reasons come to mind. One, alcohol often breaks down inhibitions. A quiet, shy person, given enough alcohol, will end up donning a lampshade at a get-together. They will become the life of the party. Of course, the next day they will be deeply embarrassed about their behavior, but at the moment of being filled with wine, they have confidence to do things they would have never had imagined themselves capable of doing —even singing in public. That's why we have karaoke bars and not karaoke schools or karaoke malls or karaoke offices. Get a few drinks in someone, and they suddenly become Paul McCartney or Celine Dion.

Two, alcohol provides an escape—though quite temporary —from the pressures of life. After a drink or two, the picture changes. The person enters "Miller Time." The bad marriage, the dead-end job, the bills, and the out-of-control children fade into the background, and life takes on a more beautiful glow. In response to that beauty, the person often breaks out into, "We are the world, we are the children . . . " or "The hills are alive with the sound of music . . ." Songs have a way of expressing feelings in a way mere words do not.

Three, alcohol often makes us more affectionate toward others. Granted, there are "mean" drunks, but many who drink suddenly become the friend of everybody. They slap you on the back and call you "old pal." I'm sure you have noticed how liquor advertisements portray people having a good time together. They want us to know how a few drinks served early in the evening can "break the ice" and induce conviviality. Before long people have their arms around one another, swaying to the music and belting out lyrics to familiar tunes.

Aldous Huxley said if he were a millionaire he would form a company of researchers to look for a substitute for alcohol. He wrote,

> If we could sniff or swallow something that would abolish inferiority, atone us with our fellows in a glowing exultation of affection, and make life in all its aspects divinely beautiful and significant, and if this heavenly, world-transforming drug were of such a kind that we could wake up next morning with a clear head and undamaged constitution, then it seems to me that all our problems would be solved and our earth would be a paradise.[2]

Paul found that "world-transforming drug" in the presence of the Holy Spirit, not alcohol. It is the Spirit who makes us more affectionate toward others, puts our problems into perspective, and drives us to song. The early church was a singing church. In Ephesians Paul contrasts two kinds of gatherings: pagan and Christian. According to Paul, wine fuels a pagan gathering (an interesting sidelight is that the Greek word for "symposium" means "drinking party"), and the Spirit fuels a Christian gathering. In Paul's analogy a pagan gathering leads to debauchery while a Christian gathering leads to praise and thanksgiving to God. Of course, we know that is not always the case. Not every non-Christian gathering leads to wickedness, and not every Christian gathering leads to praise and thanksgiving. I have been in church committee meetings and board meetings where praise and thanksgiving were the last things on people's minds, and I have been in secular settings where people out love and out serve the Christians. Nonetheless, Paul's point is clear. If you are going to get drunk on something, get drunk on the Spirit. She will not leave you with a hangover. Rather, the Spirit will make you over into all God intended you to be. She will also place a melody in your heart.

## MAKING WORSHIP A PART OF YOUR SMALL GROUP

How do you feel about adding music to your small group? How do you feel about "speaking to one another in psalms, hymns, and spiritual songs?" How do you feel about making worship a part of the group's agenda? My guess is you feel one or all of the following: uncertain, awkward, inadequate, and/or willing.

You may be uncertain about the place of worship in a small group. You have been under the impression that worship is reserved for Sunday mornings in church buildings. And in part you are right. Sanctuaries are places of worship, but not the only place to worship God. In response to the Samaritan woman's question about the proper place to worship, Jesus answered her, "The hour is coming, and is now here, when the true worshipers will worship the Father in spirit and truth, for the Father seeks such as these to worship him" (John 4:23). In other words, Jesus was telling her what matters is not *where* you worship but *where your heart is* when you worship. Worship can as easily take place in a small group as in a sanctuary or worship center.

In an article titled "God Sensitive Small Groups,"[3] Joel Comiskey recommends four staple ingredients for a healthy small group:

- Upward Focus: Knowing God through worship and prayer
- Inward Focus: Knowing each other through fellowship
- Outward Focus: Reaching out to those who don't know Christ through small group evangelism
- Forward Focus: Raising up new leaders through training and mentoring.

He claims that though no small groups are alike, good ones contain these four elements. I agree. A healthy small group lives out the great commandment by placing God at the center of its time together. It takes time to love God with all its heart, mind, and soul before it moves to loving one another.

You may feel awkward and inadequate, as well as uncertain, about practicing this particular "one another" passage of speaking to one another in psalms, hymns, and spiritual songs. You may be thinking to yourself, "I don't want to worship God in our small group because I can't sing." I can relate. I do not have the greatest singing voice. I have difficulty carrying a tune, but something happened in my small group one December that caused me to take another look at making music together.

My small group only sang once a year. Every December we would have a group Christmas party. We would each bring an item of food to share. After the scrumptious meal, we would have a devotional reading and then sing Christmas carols. We sang for a good thirty minutes, and then it hit me. If all we "non-singers" can sing Christmas carols with great joy, why can't we speak psalms, hymns, and spiritual songs with one another as well? The answer was obvious. We could.

So can you. You do not have to be musically gifted to incorporate praising God through song in your group. Remember, we are told to "make a joyful *noise* [emphasis on noise] to the Lord." What's important is not the quality of our singing but the spirit in which it is offered. If our heart is in the right place, no matter how we sound, it will be pleasing to God. If you have someone who can play the guitar or piano, all the better, but it is not necessary. Some groups use tapes or CDs to guide and accompany them. Begin with two or three familiar songs at first. Later you might want to increase the amount of time you spend singing together.

Maybe, in spite of your awkwardness and sense of inadequacy, you are willing to give this "one another" passage a try. If so, let me offer some suggestions.

## SOME SUGGESTIONS FOR SMALL GROUP WORSHIP

*First, keep your eyes on the target.*

Transformational groups center themselves in God. They seek to connect vertically (with God) and well as horizontally (with each other). In December of 2000 school kids in the United States were asked who they think is the most important person in the world today.[4] Among their rankings:

| | |
|---|---|
| The U.S President | # 1 |
| The Pope | # 2 |
| "Myself" | #11 |
| Harry Potter author, J. K. Rowling | #13 |
| God | #19 |

We may shake our heads at those responses, but we can be guilty of something similar. Sometimes God slips a little when it comes to being the most important person in a small group. If we are in the group solely for what we can get out of it, we have missed the mark. God needs to be at the core of what we do. If God is at the periphery of a group—or excluded from a group—very little transformation will take place. I think of what Jesus would later say to the Ephesian church. Some forty years after Paul had written to them, the risen Jesus appeared to the elder John on the island of Patmos and commented on the state of the church in Ephesus (Revelation 2:1-7). Jesus affirmed the church for doing many good things. He loved the way they toiled faithfully and endured patiently. He praised the church for the way they dealt with evildoers. No church produced as many good works as this church, yet Jesus threatened to remove their name from the list of "Hall of Fame" churches. Why? They had failed to keep their eyes on the target. Jesus said to them, "I have this against you, that you have abandoned the love you had at first" (Revelation 2:4). If we drift from the core, if we fail to keep our eyes on the target (Jesus Christ), we have no chance of being a "Hall of Fame" group. We may do a lot of good things together, but not the most important thing of all—loving God.

*Second, be diverse.*

Worship involves more than singing. Prayer, meditation, thanksgiving, confession, responsive readings, and devotional readings can add richness and depth to your time of worship together.

A wonderful resource to consider is *A Guide to Prayer for Ministers and Other Servants* by Rueben P. Job and Norman Shawchuck. The guide is full of invocations, scriptures, and readings for reflection, all centered around liturgical themes such as "The Cost of Discipleship," "Christ the King," "Chosen by God," and "Listen to Jesus Christ." For example, for the theme "The Power of the Gospel,"[5] the order of service goes as follows:

> I. *Invocation*
> Almighty God, may the transforming power of your gospel be at work in my life today and always. Amen.
>
> II. *2 Corinthians 12:1-10*
>
> III. *A Reading for Reflection*
> "We have not advanced very far in our spiritual lives if we have not encountered the basic paradox of freedom, to the effect that we are most free when we are bound. But not just any way of being bound will suffice; what matters is the character of our binding. The one who would like to be an athlete, but who is unwilling to discipline his body by regular exercise and by abstinence, is not free to excel on the field or the track. His failure to train rigorously and to live abstemiously denies him the freedom to go over the bar at the desired height, or to run with the desired speed and endurance. With one concerted voice the giants of the devotional life apply the same principle to the whole of life with the dictum: *Discipline is the price of freedom.*" (From *The New Man for Our Time* by Elton Trueblood)
>
> IV. *Reflection: silent and written*
>
> V. *Hymn*

That particular order of worship may or may not fit your small group's style of praising God together, but it provides a place to start, and you can modify the order to fit your group.

Another great small group worship resource is *The Small Group Idea Book* edited by Cindy Bunch. Here's a sampling of some of the material she has collected:

- *Attributes of God* by Carol Johnson. Go around the group, having each person take the next letter in the alphabet to describe an attribute of God. Psalm 145.[6]

- Devotional Readings. J. I. Packer's *Knowing God*, A.W. Tozer's *The Knowledge of the Holy*, and J. B. Phillip's *Your God Is Too Small* are excellent choices. Read short excerpts which will direct your thoughts to God.[7]

- *The Lord's Prayer* by Patty Cell. Use each line of the Lord's Prayer as a guide for a few minutes of group prayer. For example, after "hallowed be thy name" is read, worship by using various names for God in praise. Work through the entire prayer in this way.[8]

- *Worship poster* by Nina Thiel. Get a large poster board or five-foot piece of butcher paper. Bring colored markers, magazines, scissors, and glue. Have everyone gather around and make a visual representation of praise to God, each on their own "corner" of the poster. They can make a collage, draw a picture, write a verse and so on. Put it up on the wall when everyone's done.[9]

Her book contains thirty-two more creative worship suggestions. If your group needs some ideas of how to worship together, this book will be invaluable.

*Third, start slow.*

Start with a song or two or a responsive reading or a centering prayer. You might even want to read the words of a hymn and have people reflect on it before you sing together. Use familiar songs. Encourage people to think of themselves as speaking to God when they sing. Do not push people into what they might feel uncomfortable or awkward doing. As people become more comfortable, expand your time of worship.

*Fourth, involve group members.*

Assign portions of the worship service to different people. One person might lead the singing, another the time of confession, and another the reflective reading. The more people involved, the more stimulating the worship will be. Also, be aware of the gifts in the group. Some may read extremely well, and others may sing extremely well. Putting the reader in charge of singing may not be wisest course of action.

*Fifth, keep it creative.*

Doing worship the same way, week in and week out, may lead to boredom and stagnation. Take turns planning worship drawing upon each member's imaginative spirit. Some members will naturally enjoy singing more than others. Some will enjoy silence and reflection. Some will enjoy devotional readings. As a result, the worship will vary as each member places his or her thumbprint on it. Once a quarter, brainstorm about your worship time. Consider, "What works?" "What doesn't?" and "What can we do better or differently?"

John Ortberg, a teaching pastor at Willow Creek Community Church in South Barrington, Illinois, confesses,

> I need to worship.
>
> I need to worship because without it I can forget that I have a Big God beside me and live in fear. I need to worship because without it I can forget his calling and begin to live in a spirit of self-preoccupation. I need to worship because without it I lose a sense of wonder and gratitude and plod through life with blinders on. I need to worship because my natural tendency is toward self-reliance and stubborn independence.[10]

I, too, need to worship for those very same reasons, but I also need to worship with the members of my small group. I say that because of Denn Denning's doctoral dissertation. When I graduated from seminary, I was looking for a church that was big on small groups. I found one, of all places, in Omaha, Nebraska. The pastor at the time was Denn Denning. We served together for six-and-one-half years, with Denn as head of staff and me as the associate pastor overseeing small group life. One day I asked Denn about the topic of his doctoral dissertation, and Denn said, "I researched the relationship between *koinonia* (in-depth fellowship) and worship. What I discovered was this: the deeper the bonds of friendship, the greater the experience of corporate worship. If you want to make worship come alive, then get close to other folk. Love them. Pray with them. Bear their burdens. Good worship is a function of good fellowship."

In light of that, what better place to worship than with those we love the most? I love large corporate worship in a church sanctuary with hundreds of folk present. The singing is powerful. The message is inspirational. The sacraments are meaningful. But I also enjoy small group worship where three, five, or ten are gathered, and God is in our midst. Being close to people helps me to feel close to God.

Create a more God-sensitive small group. Set aside time to worship together. Speak to one another in psalms, hymns, and spiritual songs. Sing and make music in your heart to the Lord, always giving thanks to God for everything, in the name of our Lord Jesus Christ.


## GROUP DISCUSSION AND SHARING

1. **Icebreaker** (20-30 *minutes*)
   - One of my favorite songs in high school was . . .
   - A song I want sung at my funeral is . . .

2. **Discussion** (10-20 *minutes*)
   - How does the idea of adding an element of worship to your group strike you?
   - Do you agree that good fellowship leads to good worship? Why or why not?

3. **Worshiping Together** (10 *minutes*)
   As an experiment, try the following worship liturgy. At the end, discuss your thoughts and feelings about your worship experience.

I.    Begin by singing "The Doxology" in its traditional form, as below, or with the words you are familiar.

> *Praise God from whom all blessings flow;*
> *Praise God all creatures here below;*
> *Praise God above ye heavenly host;*
> *Praise Father, Son, and Holy Ghost. Amen.*

II.   Read Psalm 27 responsively alternating between leader and group.

> The Lord is my light and salvation; whom shall I fear?
>
> *The Lord is the stronghold of my life; of whom shall I be afraid?*
>
> When evildoers assail me to devour my flesh—my adversaries and foes—they shall stumble and fall.
>
> *Though an army encamp against me, my heart shall not fear; though war rise up against me, yet I will be confident.*
>
> One thing I asked of the Lord, that I will seek after: to live in the house of the Lord all the days of my life, to behold the beauty of the Lord, and to inquire in his temple.
>
> *For he will hide me in his shelter in the day of trouble; he will conceal me under the cover of his tent; he will set me high on a rock.*
>
> I believe that I shall see the goodness of the Lord in the land of the living.
>
> *Wait for the Lord; be strong, and let your heart take courage; wait for the Lord!*

III.  Observe two minutes of silence, meditating on the words of the Psalm.

IV.   Close by singing "The Doxology" once again.

4.   **Sharing** *(15-30 minutes)*
   * On a scale of 1 to 10, where would you place your comfort level when it comes to worshiping as a small group?
   * What would you like to do when it comes to worshiping in your group?
   * How can the group be praying for you in the days ahead?

5.   **Praying** *(5-10 minutes)*
   Choose a way to close in prayer

CHAPTER EIGHT

# DO NOT PROVOKE ONE ANOTHER

If we live by the Spirit, let us also walk by the Spirit.
Let us have no self-conceit, no provoking of one another,
no envy of one another.
Galatians 5:25-26 RSV

Our children knew how to push each other's buttons. They were masters at it. They took great joy in it . . . and they drove us nuts! Many a dinner conversation included such words of caution as, "Okay, Jenny, that's enough, stop picking on your brother," or "Josh, quit it. You know that upsets your sister." Even today, as adults, they can still get to one another. Jennifer, with a certain inflection in her voice, can cause her brother to blush by simply uttering the words, "I love you, Josh." In response he purses his lips, shakes his head, and tells her, "Shut up!" Josh can tweak his sister by reminding her of the time she sent a video tape to the singing group "New Kids on the Block," pledging to them her never-ending love.

When thinking of our children, two stories come to mind. I think of the teenage boy who was tormenting the family dog by doing such things as pulling a bone on a string to keep it from him, and jumping from behind a door to scare him, and covering his food with a big wire strainer to frustrate him, and pulling a pillow over the dog's head for pure spite.

His mother yelled, "Jeremy! Why are you tormenting the dog?"

Jeremy responded, "I can't find my sister!" Jeremy could have been our son.

I also think of the third grade Sunday School teacher who was giving a Bible lesson on the commandment, "Honor your father and mother." She asked, "Does anyone know a commandment for brothers and sisters?"

One child confidently raised her hand and answered, "Thou shall not kill!" That confident little girl could have been our daughter.

Experts call it "sibling rivalry." Sigmund Freud wrote, "A small child does not necessarily love his brothers and sisters . . . often he obviously does not . . . He hates them as competitors, and it is a familiar fact that his attitude persists for long years, till maturity is reached or even later, without interruption."[1] For what do siblings compete? They compete for their parent's love and affection.

When Raisa Gorbachev, the wife of the former leader of the Soviet Union, was scheduled to visit a New York City elementary school in 1988, a kindergarten teacher asked her students, "If Mrs. Gorbachev were your mother—think of her as the mom of Moscow—and you were all alone with her, what would you ask her?" Without hesitation, a little girl raised her hand and said, "I would ask her if she loves me better than my brother."

Three factors intensify sibling rivalry: the first-born factor, the family-size factor, and the same-sex factor. Think about it. Imagine little Buford, the first-born, alone with Mom and Dad. He is the center of their world. He has their undivided attention, and then along comes an intruder, his baby sister, Bertha. Bertha infringes on little Buford's turf. The parents think Bertha will be a great playmate for Buford. Buford sees it as someone stealing his parent's love. Not only that, but it's just the four of them—Mom and Dad, Buford and Bertha—and usually the smaller the family, the more intense the rivalry. Trudy and I had only two children. Maybe we should have had more to decrease the rivalry! Looking back, I am amazed at how creative my two children could be at putting one another down. Their cutting remarks almost became an art form, albeit a cruel one. Thankfully, however, they were of different sexes. If they had been of the same sex, it could have been even worse. I think of the scar my wife has on her back. She got it from her sister, Susan, who bit Trudy during one of their many childhood arguments.

All this might explain what happened between Cain and Abel, the first two siblings in the Bible. According to the biblical narrative, Cain and Abel had all three factors present in their relationship. Cain was the firstborn, and Abel was "the intruder." They came from a small family, and they were both of the same sex. Is it just a coincidence that the first recorded act of murder occurred between the first pair of siblings?

We won't ever know with certainty who or what provoked Cain. Did his parent's shower too much affection on Abel? Did they love Abel best? Did that get under Cain's skin? Or was there something about Abel that grated on Cain? Author Frederick Buechner thinks so. In *Peculiar Treasures: A Biblical Who's Who*, he writes,

> Abel was like his sheep—the same flat, complacent gaze, the thick curls low on his forehead, a voice like the creak of new shoes when he prayed. His prayers were invariably answered, his flocks fattened, and the wool fetched top price. His warts disappeared overnight. His advice to his brother was invariably excellent. Cain took it as long as he could and then he let him have it with a pitchfork . . . [2]

Or did God have something to do with it? The account reads, "And the Lord had regard for Abel and his offering, but for Cain and his offering he had no regard. So Cain was very angry and his countenance fell" (Genesis 4:4-5). Did God's delight in Abel's offering, and not Cain's offering, send Cain over the edge? We will never know.

## TWO "UN'S"

To provoke means "to make or try to make a person or animal angry or annoyed," "to cause a reaction, especially a negative one," or "to make angry, to offend; to incense; to enrage." Synonyms include words such as "bait," "enrage," "exasperate," "inflame," and "irritate." Reading the story of Cain and Abel we realize a couple of things.

*First, we realize that, at times, provoking someone is UNAVOIDABLE.*

Often times, standing for what is right and true ticks someone off. We see that in God's relationship with Cain. God had good reason to favor Abel's offering over Cain's. To say both were equally good would have been a lie. Listen to the story:

> In the course of time Cain brought to the Lord an offering of the fruit of the ground, and Abel for his part brought the firstlings of his flock, their fat portions. And the Lord had regard for Abel and his offering, but for Cain and his offering he had no regard. So Cain was very angry and his countenance fell. (Genesis 4:3-5)

Let me tell you what some folk have said in attempting to explain these verses. For example, one Old Testament scholar says this story is simply a tough lesson in God's grace. He claims there was nothing inherently better in Abel's offering than Cain's. God simply chose, as God would later choose Jacob over Esau, to favor one and not the other. We might say, "That's not fair!" but what do we say to our children when they say those words to us? We often say, "Tough, life isn't fair!" The Old Testament scholar says that is the lesson of the story: Get used to it; life is not fair. We are not to pout or question God's grace, because it is God's prerogative to call whom God wants to call and bless whom God wants to bless.

Others have said God's acceptance of the offering has nothing to do with God's freedom, but rather with worship. They say that when it comes to worship, God prefers blood offerings rather than cereal offerings. That's why God sent a Son and not a box of Wheaties to take away the sins of the world. They see this story as a tool to instruct the people of Israel on how to worship God best.

Though interesting, these arguments overlook something. The reason for the rejection and acceptance had nothing to do with God's grace or good worship. It had to do with something else. Note the word "an" in the third verse:

> In the course of time Cain brought to the Lord *an* offering of the fruit of the ground.

Cain brought *an* offering, not necessarily the best, not necessarily the finest, just *an* offering. We get the sense he brought something like brussels sprouts or lima beans. It was an offering, but it was nothing like barley or strawberries. Picture yourself in worship. The offertory is coming next, so you reach in your wallet or purse, and you have a dollar bill, a five-dollar bill, a ten-dollar bill, a twenty-dollar bill, a fifty-dollar bill, and a hundred-dollar bill. You give the five-dollars, an offering, not the best, not the finest, but *an* offering. Note what Abel gave. Note the word "firstlings" in the fourth verse:

> And Abel for his part brought the firstlings of his flock, their fatted portions.

Like the fatted calf in the prodigal son story, Abel brought nothing but the best. With Cain, we get the sense that he gave some leftovers. Granted Cain gave, but a spirit of sacrifice, a going out of one's way to honor God was not present. Abel, on the other hand, gave only the best, the fatted portions from his firstborn sheep.

Why, then, was one more acceptable than the other? I'm convinced it was a matter of attitude. Abel is the first cheerful giver in the Bible. Cain is the first reluctant one. In accepting one and not the other, God was simply being honest. One pleased God more than the other. God was attempting to teach Cain a valuable lesson—to hold things loosely—but Cain would have nothing to do with it. He chose to blame Abel rather than look at his own attitude toward giving.

Should God have been less than honest? Should God have pretended that both offerings were equally good and valuable? I do not think so. God simply communicated the truth, and the truth provoked Cain.

At times provoking others is unavoidable. For this very reason, I dreaded preaching or teaching on controversial issues. I knew that whatever position I took, whatever conclusion I had come to, would offend, incite, or exasperate someone. People would ask questions such as, "What's your position on abortion?" or "What's your position on homosexuality?" or "You don't think we should borrow money to build, do you?" or "Do you think there is really a heaven and a hell?" No matter how I answered, I knew someone's nose would get out of joint. Should I have lied to them? Should I have told them what they wanted to hear? Absolutely not. It's just that this "not provoking" business is a little more complicated than the Apostle Paul makes it out to be. Sometimes it is unavoidable.

*Second, provoking someone can be UNINTENTIONAL.*

Earlier in the chapter I quoted Frederick Buechner. He claims that Abel's very personality, his very success, grated on his brother. That may or may not have been the case, but if so, it was likely unintentional. From the little glimpse we get of Abel in the Bible, he hardly seems to be the kind of person who got up in the morning and said, "I wonder how I can get under my brother's skin this morning?" More likely, he got up in the morning and said, "I wonder how I can put a smile on God's face today?"

I have no desire to provoke others. I take that back. I might try to provoke others to do good things, but I have no desire to provoke people in a negative way. Sometimes, however, it just happens. I unintentionally set someone off. They object to the way I comb my hair, or my political affiliation, or the car I drive. In this regard my wife, Trudy, and I chuckle over her gut reaction to one of our local morning newscasters. She can't stand his voice. It gets on her nerves. She says, "Please turn to another channel for the morning news. I cannot take this guy. He bugs me." I, on the other hand, have no negative reaction whatsoever to the man. Does he intend to offend my wife? Does he get up in the morning and say, "I wonder how I can get a rise out of Trudy today?" No, he does not. It is purely unintentional. Sometimes we hook something in another's subconscious that has more to do with them than us.

Other times we unintentionally provoke by putting our foot in our mouth. We do not intend to do it; we are just being our clumsy selves. We go up to someone at church, introduce ourselves and say, "I have never met you before. Are you new here?" only to have them say in a huff, "No, I have been a member here for fifteen years." Or we ask someone whom we haven't seen for a while, "How's your husband?" to have her say with an edge in her voice, "I don't know. We divorced six months ago." Or we say, "Don't you just hate the way government employees waste our tax dollars?" only to have the person reply, "Not really. I work for the city." All of us wish life came with a rewind button that we could press for such moments.

Still other times we provoke unintentionally due to the other person's state or stage in life. For example, early in our marriage my wife was in a young mother's support group. They met every Tuesday morning throughout the school year. Trudy cherished the group and formed deep friendships, but one day she annoyed one of the women. Trudy was pregnant with our second child, and she was sharing how much she enjoyed being pregnant. She spoke in glowing terms of the sensation of the baby moving in her womb. After the group one of the women came up to her and said, "How could you be so insensitive? I am unable to get pregnant. We had to adopt our only child. I have no idea what it's like to be pregnant. Watch what you say in the future because there are others like me out there." Trudy was devastated. She had no intention of irritating the woman.

## THREE POSITIVE STEPS

While we may not be able to do much about the "un's"—the unavoidables and the unintentionals—we can do something about reducing the provocation quotient in our small group.

*One thing we can do is to deal appropriately when provoked.*

Cain failed miserably at this. We assume Cain flew off the handle and struck Abel in an instinctive reflex of anger. The story, however, does not suggest that. After Cain's encounter with God, he seethed. Later he invited his brother into the field, and while there, he killed him. In other words, it was premeditated murder. To compound matters, Cain did not show any remorse over his brother's death. When questioned about Abel's whereabouts, he answered like a snotty teenager: "Am I my brother's keeper?" If you have ever had a junior higher in your home, you know the exact tone in Cain's voice. There are certainly many different ways he could have responded. He could have dealt more responsibly with his anger.

Anger is dangerous for individuals and for groups. Because anger works up steam, it energizes, and it often throws off reasoned thinking. Judgments made under the duress of anger are often poor ones that we regret the next hour or the next day. We say and do things when irate that we would never consider when calm. I think of the children who provoked their mother to anger. After putting them to bed, she changed into old slacks and a droopy blouse and proceeded to wash her hair. As she heard her children getting more and more rambunctious, her patience grew thin. Irritated by their behavior, she threw a towel around her head and stormed into their room, putting them back to bed with stern warnings. As she left the room, she heard her three-year-old say with a trembling voice, "Who was that?"

Anger can do that: It can change us into a different, and dangerous, person. Concerning the danger, Jesus uttered these words in the Sermon on the Mount: "If you are angry with a brother or sister, you will be liable for judgment." In other words, when provoked, you stand at a crossroads. You can make matters better or worse. You can escalate the provocation or you can ease the tension. To ease the tension, consider the following "tension easer" process:

- *When provoked, instead of "flying off the handle," grab the handle.* Hold on. Do what works for you to hold yourself in check. Maybe it works to say, "Calm down, calm down" over and over to yourself before responding. Maybe it works to take a few deep breaths. Maybe it works to look for Jesus in the eyes of the provoker. Maybe it works for you to take a "two-minute time-out" before you respond. Maybe it means calling upon your mother's wisdom of "If you can't say anything nice, don't say anything at all." Whatever it takes, grab the handle. Get a hold of yourself. Fight the urge to respond immediately.

- *Second, ask, "Is this one of those times where Jesus is calling me to turn the other cheek?"* Though payback may be tempting, Jesus calls us to live by the higher law of love: to respond to the treatment we receive from others in a manner reflecting the freedom and love we find in him. Turning the other cheek is not surrender, but a strategy of operation. Such an act, if we choose to take it, takes the initiative in behaving in the freedom of Christ and his love. When provoked, we have a choice not only to respond appropriately or inappropriately, but also to decide to fight back or to let the matter go. What we decide, based on what we sense Jesus saying, will vary from one situation to the next.

- *Third, if you decide to engage the person, consider rehearsing what you are going to say.* Remember that anti-drug commercial where the parents appear to be speaking to their teenage child about drugs? The camera shows the back of a chair with the parents standing in front of the chair, speaking to their teenager. The parents conclude their "drug talk" by saying to one another, "Well, how did we do?" and the camera moves to the front of the chair, and surprise, we see a teddy bear in the chair, not a teenager. It was a dress rehearsal for the parents. They wanted to get the words right before they approached their child. Well-chosen words, rather than ill-chosen words, serve us better in the long run.

- *Finally, when provoked, guard against feeding anger.* New Testament Greek has two words for anger. One is *thumos*, which is likened to a flame that flares from dry straw. It both blazes quickly and dies down quickly. Over the years I have displayed this type of anger, especially when driving. Someone cuts me off, I respond intensely, and then the anger is gone. The other kind of anger is *ogre*, which is anger become hardened. It is long-lived anger; it's the anger a person nurses to keep it warm. The person will not let it die. The person reminds himself or herself regularly of the alleged injustice or hurt in order to keep it fresh. It's the anger of a college professor who votes "no" on a colleague's application for tenure because four years earlier the colleague voted against his curriculum initiative. It's the type of anger Cain exhibited toward Abel. Jesus comes down hard on this type of anger. He condemns anger that won't forget, refuses to be pacified, and seeks revenge.

*Another thing we can do to reduce the "provocation quotient" in our group is to learn what gets under one another's skin.*

People in my small group know I value certain group norms. When those norms are ignored, my buttons get pushed. I like to begin a group on time and end on time. If the group covenant says we will begin at 7:00 and end at 9:00, I expect to begin at 7:00 and end at 9:00. I start to go nuts when we wait for latecomers to start our meeting. I also go nuts if the group leader does not keep us on task, and we run five or ten minutes past 9:00. Also, when sharing, I like people to give us the *Readers' Digest* version not the *War and Peace* version. I do not need all the details; just give me the pertinent facts and feelings. When someone shares on and on, I begin squirming in my seat and have to battle the urge to say, "Would you just cut to the chase?"

How do we find out what gets under one another's skin? An easy way is to ask. Once a quarter I encourage small groups to take stock. I encourage them to set aside their regular study, and instead ask two questions:

- "What are three things you love about the group?"
- "What is one thing you would like to see us do differently?"

The second question helps reduce the provocation quotient. By asking this question once a quarter, a group regularly identifies those behaviors that get under each other's skin. With that knowledge in hand, the group can make adjustments in how it functions.

A more difficult, but vitally important, way to know what "gets" to people is to observe. After being in a group for a while, I learn to avoid certain subjects. I call them "Don't go there issues." I know from simple observation and experience that if I bring up particular issues, someone will get his or her nose bent out of shape. I do not avoid these subjects because I am a coward. At least, I do not think I do. I avoid them because of Paul's counsel not to provoke one another. We have been there, and we have done that, and we do not need to go there or do that again. I do not need to tell Ed how wonderful contemporary worship is because he hates it. I do not need to engage Mark in a conversation about inclusive language because he's made up his mind on that subject. I do not need to tell Margaret how I feel about hand bells because we will only get into it once again.

*Finally, in reducing the provocation quotient, commit to being a peacemaker.*

Bruce Larson relates a wonderful story about an action-packed, feeling-intensive bus ride. It was close to Christmas. He got on a crowded bus where all the seats were taken, and he had to stand. To occupy his time, he read a book as he rode. Suddenly the bus came to a quick stop, and he accidentally struck the man seated next to him. The man went nuts, despite Bruce's repeated attempts to apologize. A woman came to Bruce's defense. She told the man how difficult it was to stand while riding. Her comments only exacerbated the situation, and then she and the man got into it. A young man sitting next to the offended man tried to calm him down. He did not succeed. Suddenly someone on the bus sarcastically shouted, "Merry Christmas, everybody!"

The bus came to its next stop, and the angry man got off. Bruce took the man's seat next to the young man who had tried to calm the man down. The young man said to Bruce, "I hope you will forgive him for the way he acted. You really picked the worst possible time to tangle with him. He's a bricklayer, and today he had an accident that almost cost him his hand. The foreman threatened to fire him. Not only that, but he is having trouble with his wife."

Bruce asked if he was a friend of his. The young man shook his head. "I never saw him before. I'm a college student home for the holidays. We just happened to sit next to each other, and he told me his story."[3]

Three people attempted to be peacemakers: Bruce, the woman who came to his defense, and the young student. None of them was all that successful, but they did their best to smooth ruffled feathers. Our best efforts, also, may not always meet with success. Remember Jesus' words? "Blessed are the peacemakers for they will be called the children of God" (Matthew 5:9). Note, however, what Jesus did *not* say. He did not say, "Blessed are the *peace-lovers.*" There is a big difference between a peace-lover and a peacemaker. All of us are probably peace-lovers. We do not want any trouble. We do not want our peace disturbed. We want peaceful lives. Making peace, on the other hand, is a different matter because it may not bring peace to us. When the young Moses tried to reconcile two angry Hebrews, neither of them thanked him for his efforts (Exodus 2:13-14)! Instead they turned their anger against him, saying "Who made you ruler and judge over us?" Moses' attempt to make peace robbed him of peace! No matter the results, however, when we act as peacemakers, we reflect the work of God's Spirit in us. We look and act like children of God.

Listen to Paul's words one more time: "If we live by the Spirit, let us also walk by the Spirit. Let us have no self-conceit, no provoking of one another, no envy of one another."

Amen to that!


## GROUP DISCUSSION AND SHARING

1. **Worship** *(5-10 minutes, if so desired)*
   Based on the previous chapter, if your group decided to add a worship dimension to your time together, take five or ten minutes to worship together. Otherwise, move straight into the icebreaker.

2. **Icebreaker** *(20-30 minutes)*
   - Share a recent time someone or something got under your skin.
   - Share a recent time you got under someone's skin.

3. **Discussion** *(20-40 minutes)*
   - What do you think got under Cain's skin?
     ____ Parent's favoritism?
     ____ Abel's personality?
     ____ Cain's personality?
     ____ God's favoring Abel's offering over his?
     ____ Other?

   - What do you think of the following statements in this chapter? Do you agree or disagree with them?

     "At times, provoking someone is *unavoidable.* Often times, standing for what is right and true ticks someone off. We see that in God's relationship with Cain. God had good reason to favor Abel's offering over Cain's. To say both were equally good would have been a lie."

     "This 'not provoking' business is a little more complicated than the Apostle Paul makes it out to be. Sometimes it is unavoidable."

"Anger is dangerous for individuals and for groups. Because anger works up steam, it energizes, and it often throws off reasoned thinking. Judgments made under the duress of anger are often poor ones that we regret the next hour or the next day. We say and do things when irate that we would never consider when calm."

"After being in a group for a while, I learn to avoid certain subjects. I call them 'Don't go there issues.' I know from simple observation and experience that if I bring up particular issues, someone will get his or her nose bent out of shape. I do not avoid these subjects because I am a coward. At least, I do not think I do. I avoid them because of Paul's counsel not to provoke one another."

- What other comments would you like to make about the chapter? What material from the chapter do you think is particularly applicable to your group?

4.  **Sharing** *(15-30 minutes)*
    - Do the "taking stock" exercise mentioned in the chapter on page 115. Ask each other two questions:

        "What are three things you love about the group?"
        "What is one thing you would like to see us
            do differently?

    - Share your answers with one another. Remember this is one way of reducing the "provocation quotient" in your group.
    - How can the group be praying for you in the days ahead?

5.  **Praying** *(5-10 minutes)*
    Make sure the group takes time to pray together. Look over some of the prayer suggestions mentioned earlier in the book. Choose one of those suggestions or come up with something new.

CHAPTER NINE

# LAY DOWN YOUR LIVES FOR ONE ANOTHER

We know love by this, that he laid down his life for us—
and we ought to lay down our lives for one another.
1 John 3:16

Mark's teacher called in the middle of the afternoon. His mother answered the phone.

"Mrs. Smith, your son did something in class that surprised me so much that I thought you should know about it immediately." The mother grew worried. Her third-grader was usually well behaved.

"Nothing like this has happened in all my years of teaching," the woman continued. "This morning I was teaching a lesson on creative writing. And as I always do, I told the story of the ant and the grasshopper." She recounted the story as she had in class:

"The ant works hard all summer and stores up plenty of food. But the grasshopper plays all summer and does no work. Then winter comes. The grasshopper begins to starve because he has no food. So he begins to beg, 'Please, Mr. Ant, you have so much food. Please let me eat, too.' Then I said, 'Boys and girls, your job is to write the ending to the story.'

"Your son, Mark, raised his hand. 'Teacher, may I draw a picture?'

"I said, 'Well, yes, Mark, if you like, you may draw a picture. But first you must write the ending to the story.'

"As in all the years past, most of the students said that the ant shared his food through the winter and both the ant and the grasshopper lived. A few children wrote, "No, Mr. Grasshopper. You should have worked in the summer. Now, I have just enough food for myself." So the ant lived and the grasshopper died.'

"But your son ended the story in a way different from any other child, ever. He wrote, 'So the ant gave all of his food to the grasshopper. The grasshopper lived through the winter, but the ant died.'

"And the picture? At the bottom of the page, Mark had drawn three crosses."[1]

* * *

When I heard Mark's story, I was deeply touched. I thought to myself, "Here is a boy unlike other boys. Here is a boy who sees life through a different set of lenses. Here is a boy who either has great parents, a great Sunday School teacher, or both." I also thought, "Here is a boy who I hope never loses his love for Christ. Here is a boy much more spiritually attune than I. Here is a boy who can teach me what it means to follow Christ, and when he grows up, I would like to have in my small group!"

Eberhard Arnold, founder of the Bruderhof Communities, writes,

> In the human body, community is maintained only by the constant cycle of dying cells being replaced by new ones. In a similar way, a life of full community can take shape as an organism only where there is heroic sacrifice. Because it is an educational fellowship of mutual help and correction, of shared resources, and of work, a true community is a covenant made in free-willing surrender and sacrifice. As such it fights for the existence of the church.[2]

How does all this talk of sacrifice, surrender, and laying down one's life for one another strike you? Does it scare you? Does it confound you? Does it inspire you? Does it repulse you? Does it challenge you?

## OUR CALL TO LOVE

The call to sacrifice flows out of our call to love one another. The Apostle John writes,

> Beloved, let us love one another, because love is from God; everyone who loves is born of God and knows God. Whoever does not love does not know God, for God is love. (1 John 4:7-8)

Lloyd Ogilvie, chaplain of the United States Senate, tells of an advertisement that caught his eye a number of years ago. The ad read, "Finally—a luxury digital timepiece with your own personal message!" The ad went on to say, "Now for the first time, combine an advanced timekeeping system with your own custom message. Attract attention with this six-function watch that lights up any message in L.E.D. characters. Ideal personalized gift, incentive award, or personal message."[3]

Ogilvie went on to think about the message he might put on his watch, and he encouraged his readers to think what they would put on theirs. The watch message was limited to seventeen characters, so you had to be creative. My mind went into high gear. I thought of the messages I might put on it for myself. Ideas flowed freely. "Go Dodgers!" "God loves you!" "Think snow" (I love snow skiing). "Expect the best" (I can be somewhat of a pessimist). ""Hole in one!" (I love golf as well).

Then I started thinking about what I would put on the watch for other people if I gave it to them as a gift. For my wife, Trudy, I would put, "You Light Up My Life!" For my son, Josh, who works way too many hours, I would put, "Take Time." For Margaret Patten, a church organist who loves classical music, I would put, "Mozart Rules!" For my sister, Debbie, I would put, "Mom Loved Me Best!" For Charlie Scott, a friend who played basketball for the University of Tennessee, I would put, "Rocky Top." For Sandy Collins, my choral music director for a number of years, I would put, "Sing a New Song!" And . . . and . . . and if I were purchasing the watch for the Apostle John, I would put "Love One Another!"

John has often been called "The Apostle of Love." He not only referred to himself in his gospel as "The one whom Jesus loved," but he also preached love wherever he went. For example, tradition has it that late in his life John was asked to address the church in Ephesus. He was pushing one hundred years of age, and he was the only one of the original twelve still alive. When it came time to speak, he shuffled to the pulpit, looked over the congregation, said, "Love one another, love one another, love one another," and sat back down. Some in the crowd thought that the old man had lost it. The majority, however, knew this to be the very ethic of the Christian faith.

## OUR MODELS OF SACRIFICIAL LOVE

John, however, not only calls us to love one another, he tells us to love one another *sacrificially*. Listen to the examples he gives to us of such love:

God's love was revealed among us in this way: God
sent his only Son into the world so that we might live
through him. In this is love, not that we loved God but
that he loved us and sent his Son to be the atoning sacrifice for our sins. (1 John 4:9-10).

Note the two models of love here: the love of God for us *and* the
love of the Son.

One of the elders in our congregation, Peter Chaires, sent me
an e-mail. It contained a story of a typical Sunday morning in a church
with two teenagers rather disinterested in the entire proceeding. After
the usual singing of hymns, the pastor stood up and gave a brief introduction of a childhood friend. This friend, now an elderly man,
stepped into the pulpit and began to speak.

"A father, his son, and a friend of his son were sailing off the Pa-
cific Coast when a fast-approaching storm blocked any attempt to get
back to shore. The waves were so high that even though the father was
an experienced sailor, he could not keep the boat upright, and the
three were swept into the ocean."

The old man hesitated for a moment, making eye contact with
the two teenagers who were, for the first time since the service began,
looking somewhat interested in the story. (They probably had seen the
movie *The Perfect Storm*.) He continued.

"Grabbing a rescue line, the father had to make the most excru-
ciating decision of his life . . . to which boy would he throw the other
end of the line? Would he throw the line to his son or his son's friend?
He only had seconds to make his decision. The father knew that his
son was a Christian, and he also knew that his son's friend was not.
The agony of his decision could not be matched by the torrent of
waves. As the father yelled out, 'I love you, son!' he threw the line to
his son's friend. By the time he pulled the friend back to the capsized
boat, his son had disappeared beyond the raging swells into the black
night. His body was never recovered."

By this time the two teenagers were sitting straighter in the
pew, waiting for the next words to come out of the old man's mouth.

"The father," he continued," knew his son would step into eternity with Jesus, and he could not bear the thought of his son's friend
stepping into eternity without Jesus. Therefore, he sacrificed his son."
He said, "How great is the love of God that God should do the same
thing for us."

With that, the old man turned and sat back down as silence filled the room. Within minutes after the service ended, the two teenagers were at the old man's side. "That was a nice story," stated one of the boys, "but I don't think it was very realistic for a father to give up his son's life in hopes that the other boy would become a Christian."

"Well, you've got a point there," the old man replied, glancing down at his worn Bible. A big broad smile broadened his narrow face, and he once again looked up at the boys and said, "It sure isn't very realistic, is it? But I'm standing here today to tell you that story gives me a glimpse of what it must have been like for God to give up his Son for me. You see . . . I was that son's friend."

The Bible tells us the story of God's giving up a Son for us. So, we have our Heavenly Parent's love for us modeled in John's words. We also have another example. We have the Son's love modeled for us.

Ever wonder how Jesus felt about being an atoning sacrifice for our sins? Ever wonder how Jesus felt about giving his life for us? Well, from everything I read, he did it willingly. The Apostle Paul intimates in his letter to the Philippians that Jesus more or less volunteered for the duty. He chose to do it. He wasn't ordered to do it. He willingly chose to lay down his life for us.

Under the reign of Oliver Cromwell in seventeenth century England, a soldier was condemned to die. A public execution was to be carried out at the ringing of the curfew bell.

This soldier was engaged to a beautiful young woman who appeared before Cromwell and pleaded with him to spare her fiancé's life. But it was all in vain. Her fiancé would die that evening.

The preparations were finalized for the execution, and the city awaited the sounding of the curfew bell. When the time came, the sexton, who was old and deaf, put both hands upon the rope and pulled it with all his might. The bell, however, did not ring. He continued pulling and pulling, unaware that no sound was coming from the bell.

Unknown to all, the soldier's fiancé had climbed to the top of the belfry and wrapped herself around the tongue of the huge bell. As the sexton pulled the rope, she was smashed against the sides of the bell, her body absorbing the blows and muffling the sound. When the bell ceased to swing, she came down from the tower wounded and bleeding. The crowd watched her in awe and amazement.

Cromwell, who waited a short distance from the place of execution, was perplexed. Had his orders been defied? He demanded an explanation of why the bell had not tolled.

As Cromwell questioned his officers, the young woman was dragged before him. She cast herself at Cromwell's feet and confessed what she had done. With tears streaming down her cheeks, the young girl showed her bruised and bloodied hands. Once again, she pleaded for Crowell to spare her fiancé's life.

The display of love overwhelmed Cromwell. "Go your way, " he said. "Your lover lives. Curfew will not ring tonight."

Curfew will not ring for us because of what Jesus did for us. Bloodied and bruised, he willingly laid down his life for us.[4]

How are we to love one another? We are to love one another as God loved us. We are to love one another with a sacrificial love. Jesus said, "No one has greater love than this, to lay down one's life for one's friends" (John 15:13). John remembered Jesus' words, and he remembered Jesus doing that very thing for him.

## OUR EQUIPPER

The good news, of course, is that Jesus not only *calls* us to be sacrificial lovers, he *equips* us to be sacrificial lovers. If he did not equip us, we would be in deep weeds because we do not have that kind of love inside of us. At least, I don't have that kind of love inside of me. Sacrificial love does not come naturally to me. I am into self-preservation, not sacrifice. Wherever Christ lives, however, his love also lives. He pours his sacrificial love into our hearts.

One of the surest signs that Christ is alive and well in us is the divine ability we have to love sacrificially. I say that because loving sacrificially is not something we normally do on our own. Oh, we may possess that kind of love for a spouse or a child, but for others outside that small circle? No way! In fact, some of us may not even have that kind of love available for a spouse or a child. Take the woman who accompanied her husband to the doctor's office. After the examination, the doctor took the wife aside and said, "Unless you do the following things, your husband will surely die. Here's what you need to do. Every morning make sure he gets a good healthy breakfast. Have him come home for lunch each day so you can feed him a well-balanced meal. Make sure you feed him a good, hot dinner every night and don't overburden him with household chores. Also, keep the house spotless and clean so he doesn't get exposed to any unnecessary germs."

On the way home, the husband asked his wife what the doctor had told her. She replied, "You're going to die."

Many of us are like that woman. We don't have what it takes. On the other hand, if we begin to love one another sacrificially, that's the presence of Christ within us.

I want to let you in on a little secret. For years my staff sarcastically called me "Mr. Compassionate." Let me tell you how I got the nickname. We began each staff meeting with a relational Bible study. One week we studied the Parable of the Good Samaritan, about the man who was robbed, beaten, and left for dead, and how a priest and a Levite passed the man by without stopping to help. A Samaritan stopped to help, but not these good religious people. As the staff spoke critically of the priest and the Levite, I uttered the words they never let me forget. I said, "I think we are being overly hard on the priest and Levite. Maybe they were on their way to worship. If I were on my way to worship early on a Sunday morning, and I saw someone on the road, I probably would not stop. I would be in a real bind, weighing the benefit of stopping versus the cost of leaving people at the 8:00 AM worship service wondering where I was. I would not want to leave everyone hanging at the service, so I would use my cell phone, call 911, and get emergency services to the individual."

My staff was shocked. They said, "Our beloved pastor, Mr. Compassionate. We can see it now. One of our members is stretched out on the side of the road, and they see you coming, and their spirits are lifted, only to have them say, 'There goes Pastor Meyerrrrrrrrrr."

People on my staff playfully questioned the vitality of my faith based on my capacity to love. I know they were right. Loving others, especially sacrificially, does not come naturally to me. I have to open myself to Christ's love so that I may become a better lover. So, here's what I do to tap into that great sacrificial reservoir of Christ's love.

## TAPPING INTO THE RESERVOIR

*First, each morning I get loved up by God.*

Each morning I take some time in quiet study, devotion, and prayer. I do this to make contact with the greatest Lover of all time, Jesus Christ.

*Second, each morning I ask, "How can I be a conduit of God's love today?"*

Sometimes it's easy. I take someone to lunch. I drop in on so-and-so. I write a thank-you note. Sometimes it's not so easy. Sometimes it's downright hard. Sometimes the answer is, "Give up something you want to do and do what so-and-so wants to do." Sometimes the answer is, "Meyer, love someone you hate." In that regard, I doubt that Jesus felt warm fuzzies when he went to the cross. I doubt he felt warm fuzzies toward the people who spit on him, who whipped him, and who crushed a crown of thorns onto his head. But he chose to say, "Father, forgive them; for they do not know what they are doing" (Luke 23:34).

*The third thing I do is participate in a small group.*

A small group is a laboratory where one learns how to love. You have to sacrifice in a small group. You have to set aside time for other people in a small group. You have to listen to other people. You have to open yourself to other people and learn how to trust them with the fragile material in your life. But it is worth it. In a small group we are not only given opportunities to practice loving people who differ from us politically and theologically, but also we are often on the receiving end of a lot of love. Members of my small group regularly remind me of God's love, grace, and mercy.

## LIVING IT OUT

The call is clear: love each other sacrificially. Lay down your life for one another. But how do we put this directive into practice on a daily basis? We know we ought to do it, but opportunities as vast and dramatic as this do not regularly come into our lives. How often are we called to do what one mother did? Maybe you heard the story of the child who survived a Northwest airline plane crash on Sunday, August 16, 1987. Of the 155 people on board, she was the only one to come out alive. Her name was Cecelia. Cecelia survived because her mother, Paula Chican, unbuckled her own seat belt, got down on her knees in front of her daughter, wrapped her arms and body around Cecelia, and then would not let go. We applaud such acts of love, but truthfully, how many times in life do we get a chance to trade our life for another? How many times in life are we faced with something as dramatic as that?

In response to that question, C. H. Dodd writes,

> There were occasions in the life of the early church, as there are certainly tragic occasions at the present day, for a quite literal obedience to this precept [i.e., to lay down our life for others]. But not all life is tragic; and yet the same principle of conduct must apply all through. Thus it may call for the simple expenditure of money we might have spent upon ourselves, to relieve the need of someone poorer. It is, after all, the same principle of action, though at a lower level of intensity: it is the willingness to surrender that which has value for our own life, to enrich the life of another. If such a minimum response to the law of charity, called for by such an everyday situation is absent, then it is idle to pretend we are within the family of God, the realm in which love is operative as principle and the token of eternal life. [5]

Nice words will never take the place of good deeds, and all the talk in the world will never take the place of kindly action made in a spirit of self-denial and self-sacrifice. Talk is cheap. Love is not just a special way of feeling; it is an orientation of life and action. How do we exhibit such a spirit in a small group? Allow me to offer some prescriptive guidance.

One way we exhibit such a spirit is by sacrificing our personal privacy and images of adequacy. We lay down our lives by sharing what we've been through and what we are facing right now. We come clean. We articulate our struggles. We take off the mask. We let people know who we are. I like the way one person put it: "We lock people in a prison of self-doubt if we create the impression we have it all together. No one has!"[6] In order to release people from that "prison," we let them see us "warts and all." We sacrifice our personal privacy and images of adequacy. Every time a small group meets, we face a decision. "Will I lay down my need for privacy? Will I lay down my need to look good? Will I let people see the real me?"

A second way we exhibit a spirit of sacrifice in a small group relates to money and possessions. The verse that immediately follows the directive to lay down our lives for one another reads as follows: "How does God's love abide in anyone who has the world's goods and sees a brother or sister in need and yet refuses help?" (1 John 3:17). The answer to that question is obvious. God's love doesn't.

Listen to Luke's description of the early church: "All who believed were together and had all things in common; they would sell their possessions and goods and distribute the proceeds to all, as any had need" (Acts 2:44-45). How well does that describe a typical small group? How well does a typical small group meet one another's material needs? My guess is, not well.

The story is told of whole armies of Franks who, before they went into battle, were given baptism at one stroke. Many soldiers, however, went into the water with their right hand held high so they would not get wet. Then they could say, "This hand has never been baptized," and they could swing their swords and axes just as freely as ever. The modern counterpart is seen in many who have been baptized, except for their wallet. They held these high above the water.

Commenting on the rampant individualism and consumerism of the American culture, Randy Frazee writes,

> In many other parts of the world the idea of success is a quiet dinner with friends, telling stories and sharing life together. In America the idea of success is accumulating more things. The former strategy leads people toward community, whether it is based on Christian principles or not; the latter strategy leads people away from community in pursuit of working longer hours to earn more money so you can purchase that thing that promises commitment—but, of course, it never delivers.[7]

Listen to what most Americans identify as "the good life." In 1975 Roper pollsters asked people to define "the good life." Thirty-eight percent chose "a lot of money," and an identical 38 percent identified "a job that contributes to the welfare of society." They asked the same question in 1996. Those who wanted to contribute to the welfare of society dipped to 32 percent, while those who wanted "a lot of money" soared to 63 percent. Other elements of the good life included a vacation home (19 percent in 1975 and 43 percent in 1996), a second color TV (10 percent to 34 percent), a swimming pool (14 percent to 36 percent), a second car (30 percent to 45 percent), travel abroad (30 percent to 44 percent), and "really nice" clothes (36 percent to 48 percent).[8] Francis Schaeffer, twentieth-century theologian and apologist, once said that what drives Americans is a desire for affluence and personal peace.[9] He hit the nail on the head.

Are we willing to sacrifice our need for affluence, money, and possessions for the needs of others in our group? Are we willing to forego a European vacation to help someone in our group pay her rent? Are we willing to put off buying a new car to help someone send his child to college? Are we willing to open the extra bedroom in our home to someone who badly needs a place to live? Are we willing to spend less on our wardrobe so someone can go and visit an ill relative? Are we willing to create and contribute to a small group "emergency fund" to help one another when a crisis strikes? Or is it every person for himself or herself when it comes to financial matters in the group?

Picture a group of ants finding their way to a picnic and individually beginning to take crumbs several times their size back to their colony. As the ants take the crumbs away, however, they encounter a problem. They can't carry the crumbs across a large crack in the pavement. There is soon a crowd of ants with crumbs on one side of the crack with no way of continuing. After carefully surveying the problem, the ants come up with a solution. Some of the ants walk into the crack and lay their bodies down and form a bridge for the others.

Every now and again the burdens of life become unwieldy, and we do not know how we will make it. Sometimes those heavy burdens are emotional, and sometimes they are spiritual. Sometimes they are physical, and sometimes they are financial. At times like these we need others to lay their bodies down for us so we can make it to the other side. I hope you have people who will do that for you in your small group.

"No one has greater love than this, to lay down one's life for one's friends."


## GROUP DISCUSSION AND SHARING

1.  **Worship** *(5-10 minutes, if so desired)*

2.  **Icebreaker** *(15-20 minutes)*
    - Share a time when someone gave up something important for you.
    - Share a time when you gave up something important for someone else.

3.  **Discussion** *(20-30 minutes)*

    - How does the talk about laying down your life for
      another strike you? Do you find it:
        - \_\_\_\_ Repulsive
        - \_\_\_\_ Scary
        - \_\_\_\_ Inspiring
        - \_\_\_\_ Impossible
        - \_\_\_\_ Challenging
        - \_\_\_\_ Other
    - On a scale of 1 to 10, how would you rank the mes-
      sage of this chapter? Why that number?
    - How will you put this "one another" passage into
      practice in your small group?

4.  **Sharing** *(15-30 minutes)*

    - Where I sense God calling me to practice sacrificial
      love outside our group is . . .
    - Where I need the group to be praying for me is . . .

5.  **Praying** *(5-10 minutes)*

# Notes

## Chapter 1: Belong to One Another

1. Robert D. Putnam, *Bowling Alone: The Collapse and Revival of American Community* (New York: Simon & Schuster, 2000), 288.
2. Ibid. 327.
3. Ibid. 331.
4. Ibid. 304.
5. Ibid. 304.
6. As quoted by Carol Ann Fleming, "Can These Bones Live?" Thompson Scholar Program, Columbia Seminary, April 1993, 4.
7. As quoted by Robert Bellah, et al., *Habits of the Heart: Individualism and Commitment in American Life* (Berkeley: University of California, 1985), 233.
8. As quoted by John Bartlett, *Familiar Quotations* (Boston: Little, Brown and Company, 1968), 930b.
9. Robert Bellah, *Habits of the Heart: Individualism and Commitment in American Life* (Berkeley: University of California, 1985), 233.
10. Joke Distribution Network, joke.network@juno.com.
11. As quoted by Larry Krieder, *Bottom-Line Faith* (Wheaton, IL: Tyndale, 1995), 61.
12. As quoted by David Sylvester, *Great Stories* (Amarillo, TX: Today's Pulpit Publishing Company), July-September 2000, 3.
13. Robert L. Short, *The Parables of Peanuts* (New York: Harper & Row, 1968), 263.
14. Adapted from Steven A. Beebe and John T. Masterson, *Communicating in Small Groups: Principles and Practices* (New York: Longman, 2000), 73.

## Chapter 2: Be Devoted to One Another

1. Eugene Peterson, *The Message* (Colorado Springs, CO: NavPress, 1993), 329.
2. George Bush, *All My Best, George Bush* (New York: Scribner, 1999), 76.
3. Bill Gothard, as summarized in "Levels of Friendship," *The Pastor's Story File* (Platteville, CO: Saratoga Press, June 1998), 7.
4. Mitch Albom, *Tuesdays with Morrie* (New York: Doubleday, 1997), 52.
5. "Priorities," *The Pastor's Illustration Service*, (Ventnor, NJ: Pastor's Illustration Service) Volume 12, Number 1, 9.
6. As quoted in "Attitude," *Leadership: A Practical Journal for Church Leaders* (Carol Stream, IL: Christianity Today), Winter 1998, 71.
7. Larry Kreider, *Bottom Line Faith* (Wheaton, IL: Tyndale House, 1995), 125.
8. Robert Wuthrow, *Sharing the Journey: Support Groups and America's New Quest for Community* (New York: The Free Press, 1994), 305-306.
9. As quoted by William Safire & Leonard Safire, *Good Advice* (New York: Times Books, 1982), 130.
10. Lloyd J. Ogilvie, *Congratulations God Believes in You!* (Waco, TX: Word Books, 1980), 79.
11. As quoted by Henri J. M. Nouwen, *The Genesee Diary: Report from a Trappist Monastery* (Garden City, NY: Image Books, 1981), 138.

## Chapter 3: Speak Truthfully with One Another

1. Adapted and expanded from William Barclay, *The Ten Commandments for Today* (San Francisco: Harper & Row, 1973), 189-192.
2. Wetherall Johnson, *Created for Commitment* (Wheaton, IL: Tyndale House, 1989), 100.
3. As quoted in John Bartlett, *Bartlett's Famous Quotations* (Boston: Little, Brown and Company, 1968), 822.
4. William Barclay, *The Ten Commandments for Today* (San Francisco: Harper & Row, 1973), 184.
5. Paul Brand & Philip Yancey, *Fearfully and Wonderfully Made* (Grand Rapids, MI: Zondervan, 1980), 77-79.
6. M. Scott Peck, *The Different Drum: Community-Making and Peace* (New York: Simon & Schuster, 1987), 57, 59.
7. John Claypool, *The Preaching Event* (Waco, TX: Word, 1980), 75.
8. In a letter in Max Lenz (ed.), *Briefwechel mit Bucer, Vol. 1,* cited by Sissela Bock, "Lying," *Cambridge Survey Research,* (New York: Vintage, 1979), xviii.

## Chapter 4: Do Not Grumble Against One Another

1. Alan Loy McGinnis, *The Power of Optimism* (San Francisco: Harper and Row, 1990), 134.
2. Os Guinness, as quoted in *The Pastor's Story File* (Platteville, CO: Saratoga Press), August 1997, 2.
3. Denis Waitley, *Seeds of Greatness* (New York: Pocket Books, 1983), 188.
4. As quoted by Stephen Brown, "The Difficulty of Acceptance," *Key Life Network,* July-August 1992, Vol. 7, #4 (Key Biscayne, FL: Key Life), 3.
5. As quoted in "Wilt's Wish: One Woman," *Leadership: A Practical Journal for Church Leaders,* Winter 2000, (Carol Stream, IL: Christianity Today), 75.
6. As quoted by William Willimon, *Reading with Deeper Eyes* (Nashville: Upper Room Books, 1998), 77.
7. C.S. Lewis, *Experiment in Criticism* (New York: Cambridge University Press, 1961), 94.
8. Adapted from "Inspirations," www.inspirations.za.net.

## Chapter 5: Agree with One Another

1. Eugene Peterson, *The Message* (Colorado Springs: NavPress, 1993), 338.
2. Richard B. Hays, *First Corinthians: Interpretation - A Bible Commentary for Teaching and Preaching* (Louisville: John Knox Press, 1997), 23.
3. Martin R. Bartel, "Super Separation," *The Pastor's Story File,* September, 1997 (Platteville, CO: Saratoga Press), 3.

## Chapter 6: Look Out for One Another

1. Dale Bruner, *Matthew, A Commentary Volume 2* (Waco, TX: Word, 1990), 796.
2. L. Robert Keck, *Sacred Quest* (West Chester, PA: Chrysalis Books, 2000), 176.
3. Morton Kelsey, *Companions on the Inner Way* (New York: Crossroad, 1984), 138ff.
4. Bruce Larson, *The Communicator's Commentary: Luke* (Waco, TX: Word Books, 1983), 184.

5. Jill Briscoe, "Loving God with All Your Heart" *Preaching Today* (Carol Stream, IL: Christianity Today), Tape No. 84.

6. Freeman Patterson, *Photography and the Art of Seeing* (Philadelphia: Chilton Books, 1965), 9.

7. *Alcoholics Anonymous* (New York: Alcoholics Anonymous World Services, 1984), 61.

8. Told by Donald O. Maddox, "May Take Longer," *Parables, Etc.*, January 1992, (Platteview, CO: Saratoga Press), 7.

9. Steven A. Beebe & John T. Masterson, *Communicating in Small Groups* (New York: Addison Wesley Longman, 2000), 77-78.

10. Randy Frazee, *The Connecting Church* (Grand Rapids: Zondervan, 2001), 49.

# Chapter 7: Speak to One Another with Psalms, Hymns, and Spiritual Songs

1. Norman Vincent Peale, *A Guide to Confident Living* (New York: Prentice-Hall, 1948), 94-95.

2. As quoted by A. Leonard Griffith, *Ephesians: A Positive Affirmation* (Waco, TX: Word Books, 1976), 103.

3. Joel Comiskey, "God Sensitive Small Groups" May 2001, SmallGroups.com.

4. "Who's It All About," *Leadership: A Practical Journal for Church Leaders*, Spring 2001 (Carol Stream, IL: Christianity Today), 13.

5. Rueben P. Job & Norman Shawchuck, *A Guide to Prayer for Ministers and Other Servants* (Nashville: The Upper Room, 1983), 225-226.

6. Cindy Bunch, editor, *Small Group Idea Book* (Downers Grove, IL: InterVarsity Press, 1996), 48.

7. Ibid, 51.

8. Ibid, 58.

9. Ibid, 61.

10. John Ortberg, *If You Want to Walk on Water, You've Got to Get Out of the Boat* (Grand Rapids, MI: Zondervan, 2001), 196.

## Chapter 8: Do Not Provoke One Another

1. As quoted by Judith Viorst, *Necessary Losses* (New York: Simon & Schuster, 1986), 84.

2. Frederick Buechner, *Peculiar Treasures: A Biblical Who's Who* (San Francisco: Harper & Row, 1979), 19-20.

3. Bruce Larson, *30 Days to a New You* (Garden Grove, CA: Special Hour of Prayer Edition, 1994), 126.

## Chapter 9: Lay Down Your Lives for One Another

1. As told by Brad Walden, "Go the Ant, Consider His Ways" (Carol Stream, IL: *Leadership: A Practical Journal for Church Leaders*, Spring 2001), 71.

2. Eberhard Arnold, *Why We Live in Community* (Farmington, PA: Plough Publishing House, 1995), 18.

3. Lloyd John Ogilvie, *When God First Thought of You* (Waco, TX: Word, 1978), 129.

4. Steven J. Lawson, *Absolutely Sure* (Sisters, OR: Multnomah Press, 1999), 87.

5. As quoted by William Barclay, *The Daily Bible Study Series: The Letters of John and Jude*, (Philadelphia: Westminster Press, 1960), 99-100.
6. Lloyd John Ogilvie, *When God First Thought of You* (Waco, TX: Word, 1978), 103.
7. Randy Frazee, *The Connecting Church* (Grand Rapids, MI: Zondervan, 2001), 183.
8. Robert D. Putnam, *Bowling Alone: the Collapse and Revival of American Community* (New York: Simon & Schuster, 2000), 273.
9. Francis Schaeffer, "The Age of Personal Peace and Affluence," *How Then Shall We Live*, Video Series, Tape III, (Rochester, MN: L'Abri Fellowship).

# Bibliography

## BOOKS AND COMMENTARIES

Albom, Mitch, *Tuesdays with Morrie.* New York: Doubleday, 1997.

*Alcoholics Anonymous.* New York: Alcoholics Anonymous World Services, 1984.

Arnold, Eberhard, *Why We Live in Community.* Farmington, PA: Plough Publishing House, 1995.

Barclay, William, *The Ten Commandments for Today.* San Francisco: Harper & Row, 1973.

_____ . *The Daily Bible Study Series: The Letters of John and Jude.* Philadelphia: Westminster Press, 1960.

Bartlett, John, *Familiar Quotations.* Boston: Little, Brown and Company, 1968.

Beebe, Steven A. and Masterson, John T., *Communicating in Small Groups: Principles and Practices.* New York: Longman, 2000.

Bellah, Robert, et al., *Habits of the Heart: Individualism and Commitment in American Life.* Berkeley: University of California, 1985.

Brand, Paul and Yancey, Philip, *Fearfully and Wonderfully Made.* Grand Rapids, MI: Zondervan, 1980.

Bruner, Dale, *Matthew, A Commentary.* Waco, TX: Word, 1990.

Buechner, Frederick, *Peculiar Treasures: A Biblical Who's Who.* San Francisco: Harper & Row, 1979.

Bunch, Cindy, ed. *Small Group Idea Book.* Downers Grove, IL: InterVarsity Press, 1996.

Bush, George, *All My Best, George Bush.* New York: Scribner, 1999.

Claypool, John, *The Preaching Event.* Waco, TX: Word, 1980.

Frazee, Randy, *The Connecting Church.* Grand Rapids, MI: Zondervan, 2001.

Griffith, Leonard A., *Ephesians: A Positive Affirmation.* Waco, TX: Word Books, 1976.

Hays, Richard B., *First Corinthians: Interpretation-A Bible Commentary for Teaching and Preaching.* Louisville: John Knox Press, 1997.

Job, Rueben P., and Shawchuck, Norman, *A Guide to Prayer for Ministers and Other Servants.* Nashville: The Upper Room, 1983.

Johnson, Wetherall A., *Created for Commitment.* Wheaton, IL: Tyndale House, 1982.

Keck, Robert L., *Sacred Quest.* West Chester, PA: Chrysalis Books, 2000.

Kelsey, Morton, *Companions on the Inner Way.* New York: Crossroad, 1984.

Krieder, Larry, *Bottom-Line Faith.* Wheaton, IL: Tyndale, 1995.

Larson, Bruce, *30 Days to a New You.* Garden Grove, CA: Special Hour of Power Edition, 1994.

_____ , *The Communicator's Commentary: Luke,* Waco, TX: Word Books, 1983.

Lawson, Steven J., *Absolutely Sure,* Sisters, OR: Multnomah Publishers, 1999.

Lewis, C.S., *Experiment in Criticism*. New York: Cambridge University Press, 1961.

McGinnis, Alan Loy, *The Power of Optimism*. San Francisco: Harper & Row, 1990.

Nouwen, Henri J. M., *The Genesee Diary: Report from a Trappist Monastery*. Garden City, NY: Image Books, 1981.

Ogilvie, Lloyd John, *Congratulations God Believes in You!* Waco, TX: Word Books, 1980.

_____ . *When God First Thought of You*. Waco, TX: Word, 1978.

Ortberg, John, *If You Walk on Water, You've Got to Get Out of the Boat*. Grand Rapids, MI: Zondervan, 2001.

Peale, Norman Vincent, *A Guide to Confident Living*. New York: Prentice-Hall, 1948.

Patterson, Freeman, *Photography and the Art of Seeing*. Philadelphia: Chilton Books, 1965.

Peck, Scott M., *The Different Drum: Community-Making and Peace*. New York: Simon & Schuster, 1987.

Peterson, Eugene, *The Message*. Colorado Springs, CO: NavPress, 1993.

Putnam, Robert D., *Bowling Alone: The Collapse and Revival of American Community*. New York: Simon & Schuster, 2000.

Safire, William and Safire, Leonard, *Good Advice*. New York: Times Books, 1982.

Short, Robert, *The Parables of Peanuts*. New York: Harper & Row, 1968.

Viorst, Judith, *Necessary Losses*. New York: Simon & Schuster, 1986.

Waitley, Denis, *Seeds of Greatness*. New York: Pocket Books, 1983.

Willimon, William, *Reading with Deeper Eyes*. Nashville: Upper Room Books, 1998.

Wuthrow, Robert, *Sharing the Journey: Support Groups and America's Quest for Community*. New York: The Free Press, 1994.

## ARTICLES

"Attitude," *Leadership: A Practical Journal for Church Leaders*. Carol Stream, IL: Christianity Today, Winter 1998.

Bartel, Martin R., "Super Separation," *The Pastor's Story File*. Platteville, CO: Saratoga Press, September 1997.

Bock, Sissela, "Lying," *Cambridge Survey Research*. New York: Vintage, 1979.

Brown, Stephen, "The Difficulty of Acceptance," *Key Life Network*. Key Biscayne, FL: Key Life, July-August 1992.

Fleming, Carol Ann, "Can These Bones Live?" Thompson Scholar Program, Columbia Seminary, April 1993.

Gothard, Bill, "Levels of Friendship," *The Pastor's Story File*. Platteville, CO: Saratoga Press, June 1998.

Guinness, Os, "Halo Misfit," *The Pastor's Story File*. Platteville, CO: Saratoga Press, August 1997.

Maddox, Donald O. "May Take Longer." *Parables, Etc*. Platteville, CO: Saratoga Press, January 1992.

"Priorities," *The Pastor's Illustration Service.* Ventnor, NJ: Pastor's Illustration Service, Volume 12, Number 1.

Sylvester, David, "Atonement/Self-sufficiency," *Great Stories,* Amarillo, TX: Today's Pulpit Publishing House, July-September 2000.

Walden, Bruce, "Go to the Ant, Consider His Ways," *Leadership: A Practical Journal for Church Leaders.* Carol Stream: IL: Christianity Today, Spring 2001.

"Who's It All About," *Leadership: A Practical Journal for Church Leaders.* Carol Stream, IL: Christianity Today, Spring 2001.

"Wilt's Wish: One Woman," *Leadership: A Practical Journal for Church Leaders.* Carol Stream, IL: Christianity Today, Winter 2000.


## TAPES

Briscoe, Jill, "Loving God with All Your Heart," *Preaching Today*, Tape No. 84. Carol Stream, IL: Christianity Today.

Schaeffer, Francis, "How Then Shall We Live" Video Series, Rochester, MN: L'Abri Fellowship.


## INTERNET

Comiskey, Joel, "God Sensitive Small Groups," SmallGroups.com. May 2001. Joke Distribution Network, .

RICHARD C. MEYER served the church in pastoral ministry for 25 years. He has pastored small (250 members), medium (800 members), and large (1275 members) congregations in the Presbyterian church. In the fall of 2000, he left pastoral ministry to follow his passion of calling people into deep spiritual community through small groups. He currently is devoting his energies to the formation of The One Anothering Institute, a consulting resource for churches.

Meyer is a much sought-after conference speaker and small group consultant, chairperson of the Faith at Work Board, and a regular columnist for the *Faith @ Work Magazine.* His *One Anothering* series, of which this third volume is the culmination, has been called "the best book on church groups I have ever seen!"

# The ONE ANOTHERING Series
## by Richard C. Meyer

| ONE ANOTHERING VOLUME 1 | ONE ANOTHERING VOLUME 2 | ONE ANOTHERING VOLUME 3 |
|---|---|---|
| **Biblical Building Blocks for Small Groups** | **Building Spiritual Community in Small Groups** | **Creating Significant Spiritual Community** |
| ISBN 1-880913-35-6 PB 12.95 | ISBN 1-880913-73-3 PB 12.95 | ISBN 1-880913-56-9 PB 12.95 |

**ONE ANOTHERING VOLUME 1**

- Fellowship with One Another
- Love One Another
- Pray for One Another
- Care for One Another
- Bear One Another's Burdens
- Encourage and Build Up One Another
- Submit to One Another
- Admonish One Another
- Spur One Another on Toward Love and Good Deeds
- Covenant with One Another

**ONE ANOTHERING VOLUME 2**

- The Power of Community
- Meet Together
- Accept One Another
- Serve One Another
- Be Kind to One Another
- Teach One Another
- Live in Harmony with One Another
- Forgive One Another
- Do Not Envy One Another
- Be Hospitable to One Another
- Honor One Another

**ONE ANOTHERING VOLUME 3**

- Belong to One Another
- Be Devoted to One Another
- Speak Truthfully with One Another
- Do Not Grumble Against One Another
- Look Out for One Another
- Speak to One Another with Psalms, Hymns, and Spiritual Songs
- Do Not Provoke One Another
- Lay Down Your Lives for One Another

---

**Practical guides for small groups in the church that encourage people to discover one another's differing views and unique gifts. Each chapter focuses on a "one another" statement written to the early Christian church.**

---

## ~Spiritual Classics that Call to the Deep Heart's Core~
## From Innisfree Press

Available from your favorite bookseller or from Innisfree Press.

Visit our web site at www.InnisfreePress.com or call 800-367-5872 for a free catalog.

# More Books for Biblical Study

## LEADING LADIES
### Transformative Biblical Images for Women's Leadership
**JEANNE L. PORTER**
Empowerment from biblical women for women's leadership.
ISBN 1-880913-45-3 PB 13.95

## THE CALL TO THE SOUL
### Six Stages of Spiritual Development
**MARJORY ZOET BANKSON**
A framework for understanding life transitions.
ISBN 1-880913-34-8 PB 14.95

## THE GOD BETWEEN US
### A Spirituality of Relationships
**LYN BRAKEMAN**
Uncovering the mysterious ways God is present in relationships.
ISBN 1-880913-54-2 PB 14.95

## SEASONS OF FRIENDSHIP
### Naomi and Ruth as a Model for Relationship
**MARJORY ZOET BANKSON**
Valuing the gifts of different relationships in changing seasons of life.
REV. ED. ISBN 1-880913-58-5 PB 14.95

## SPIRITUAL LEMONS
### Biblical Women, Irreverent Laughter, and Righteous Rage
**LYN BRAKEMAN**
How *did* biblical women feel about their lives? A midrash view.
ISBN 1-880913-22-4 PB 12.95

## BRAIDED STREAMS
### Esther as a Model for Wholeness
**MARJORY ZOET BANKSON**
Integrating the vocational, sexual, and spiritual streams of life.
REV. ED. ISBN 1-880913-59-3 PB 14.95

## PRACTICING YOUR PATH
### A Book of Retreats for an Intentional Life
**HOLLY WHITCOMB**
One-day retreats on 7 spiritual disciplines for individuals or groups.
ISBN 1-880913-53-4 PB 15.95

## JUST A SISTER AWAY
### A Womanist Vision of Women's Relationships in the Bible
**RENITA WEEMS**
A classic on the links between women today and their biblical sisters.
ISBN 0-931055-52-0 PB 12.95

## ~Spiritual Classics that Call to the Deep Heart's Core~ From Innisfree Press

Available from your favorite bookseller or from Innisfree Press.

Visit our web site at www.InnisfreePress.com or call 800-367-5872 for a free catalog.